I AM BRAVE.
I AM STRONG.
I AM KIND.

Kristin Snow

ISBN 978-1-64299-300-4 (paperback)
ISBN 978-1-64299-302-8 (hardcover)
ISBN 978-1-64299-301-1 (digital)

Christian Faith Publishing, Inc.
832 Park Avenue
Meadville, PA 16335
www.christianfaithpublishing.com

Printed in the United States of America

Introduction

I WRITE THIS BOOK TO you as a lover and follower of Jesus. Writing this has been a journey walking through my life, realizing that the Lord has always been there holding out His right hand to mine to show me how much He loves me, to guide me, to give me strength, to help me, to guard me, and to give me rest. "Because you are my help, I sing in the shadow of your wings. I cling to you; your right hand upholds me" (Psalm 63:7–8). These words are what the Lord has shown to me to help me to grow closer to Him. Life is hard, and sometimes it seems insurmountable. It is only when I realize what I have inside me as a child of God that I am able to overcome my circumstances and live the life I am meant to live in Him.

My life was much different before I started this journey of truly following Jesus and not just "believing" in Him. I was a "mediocre" Christian trying to keep up with the hustle of this life and in turn always trying to "keep up with Jesus." I was in a cycle of not being "good enough" and then feeling like a failure, and then that same cycle repeating all over again and again. I did not feel as though I was brave enough to walk with faith and overcome my circumstances. I wasn't brave enough to follow Him and trust Him with my life. I did not know the same strength that was exhibited throughout the Bible was also mine. I felt that there was no way that I could be kind to those that hurt me, failed me, and needed my forgiveness.

I heard all these other followers that talked about the Holy Spirit speaking to them and how they lived out His will and I wanted that too. I saw them walking in faith with bravery. I saw them being strong in the midst of awful circumstances. I saw them being kind when no one deserved it. I saw that they looked different, talked different, and loved differently than others I had known. I realized that

I had someone all along that did life differently than most everyone around me. That person was my grandma, Dorothy. I wanted to live life like she did. She held out her hand to me and began to teach me how to take the hand of Jesus. She taught me that as a born-again child of God He has given me truths in His word, godly friends to guide me, and tough circumstances to help me trust Him and believe that I am victorious through Him. With her and the hand of Jesus, I learned to be brave, I learned to be strong and I learned to be kind. And if you are anything like me, you might want that too.

I can only hope and pray that this book might help you to see who you were created to be, thus making you well aware of what you hold inside of you as a child of His. I hope that what you read will make you swell with so much gratitude that you change your life to serve only Him. I hope that you don't take my word for any of it, but that you go to your Bible and read every verse I bring up. Stop and see what He is speaking to you through it. Read before the verse and after the verse to get a picture of what He is saying. It might not be the same thing that it said to me, and that's okay. I want you to start to *know* Him for yourself and not for the reasons that someone else knows Him.

I want you to live the life that He has for you. I want you to live in His will: to know that He will equip you to walk the path that He has for you. I want you to rest in His shadow: to know how to find comfort solely in Him. I want you to know you are victorious: to figure out how to embrace the victory over the enemy's lies! I want you to know how much you are loved: to see that He gave it all for you, and that alone is how He defines His love for you. I want you to know that you are brave, that you have the ability to be courageous in whatever circumstance you are in and wherever He asks you to walk. I want you to know that you are strong, that you are able to take the hand of God and conquer any and all fear. I want you to know that you are kind, that you are able to express your love for *everyone* through your actions and words. I just want you to know who you really are. That is my hope for you.

I have been praying for you.

The Wave

Save me, O God,
for the waters have come up to my neck.
I sink in the miry depths,
where there is no foothold.
I have come into the deep waters;
the floods engulf me.
I am worn out calling for help;
my throat is parched.
My eyes fail,
looking for my God.
(Psalm 69:1–3, NIV)

A WAVE OF DESPERATION HAD overcome my life. I saw it rolling in over the distance. I felt the breeze pick up the closer it came. I had felt waves like this before, but by the time they came to me on the shore, they had died out. This was different now; I was standing out in the water a few yards from the shore. I knew the wave would hit me, but I had no idea how far it would knock me back. I had no idea what it would do to my life. The wind was crisp as it bounced off my cheek and fluttered away behind me. I turned around and saw it go, like it also wanted nothing to do with this storm ahead. All the times I came out here in the water before, I chose it myself, not knowingly I suppose, but I chose it nonetheless. In the past, I could see the shore and the Lord was standing there, beckoning me back. I would choose just a few more steps out, another wave would hit me, and I would give up and come back, safe in His arms again. I'm sure we all do this I imagine; we think for a

5

moment that we can do it on our own, that we can withstand the current in a raging sea. *I'm just a few feet from shore, right? There are so many other people out here looking like they enjoy the waves.* This time was so different. The Lord brought me out here in the waters. He asked me to come with Him. When we started off the shore, it was warm and the water was nice. He was taking me out as we walked on, deeper and deeper. I felt the sand turn hard under my feet. The wind was slicing my skin as we walked; it was so cold now. The water was just a little higher than my waist now. I stopped in the faintly illuminated darkness. Stone cold, I turned to face the mountain of water coming straight for me.

There was a wave, bigger than the sunrise I watch every morning and taller than the tallest oak tree. I looked up at Him and expected Him to stop it. I realized just in that instant I had never taken His hand in mine, but it was too late. Sheer terror spread across my face when I realized what I hadn't done. In what seemed like slow motion, I felt the wind pick up. I felt the mist on my face as the water came closer. I felt the sand swirling around my legs under me. I stood there, paralyzed in the middle of my circumstance. I didn't even try to scream. The wave plowed into me and plunged me under the water. It slammed me off the bottom where my feet just minutes ago had been standing. My head ricocheted off the rock-solid seafloor. I was sure I was bleeding everywhere. I was so scared I didn't know which way was up. I was kicking everywhere, trying to open my eyes long enough to see light. The current was dragging me from the shallows into deep, cold, black water.

I went into sheer panic. I couldn't breathe and my lungs ached for the air I knew existed just a few feet away. My body needed the oxygen that I just couldn't supply. My hands were flailing, trying to grab onto anything that would make me stop moving. I was ripping through the water going nowhere. Nothing about knowing how to swim would come in handy here at the bottom of defeat. As soon as I was sure that I was going up, a current would laugh at me and suck me deeper down. Just as I thought in that instant I wouldn't come back up, just as I lost my last wave of real hope, a fierce hand grabbed my arm and pulled me up out of the miry depths. He had to have been watching me the whole time to know where I was in this blackness. His grip was so strong I could feel it making marks on my arm. It was powerful and sure. I saw the light coming closer to my face. I broke through the glass pane of water and gasped for any air I could suck in. He stood me up on my feet right where we stood before the wave. I held a steady grip on His hand. I swore to myself I would never let go. I wiped the water from my face with my free hand and shook the fear from my insides. I looked up at Him: *Why did you bring me here? Why would you let that happen? It would have been so easy for you to grab my hand before it hit.* I could feel He wanted to show me something, but He never said a word. I looked up, astonished.

There were people swimming all around me; I never noticed them as we were walking out here before I was dragged under. They didn't know at this moment that we were there. Some were laughing, some were scared, and many were confused. Some I could tell had been here a long time by the lackluster in their eyes. Some were drowning in the water just above their noses. They had been swimming so long and they were so tired. They were used to these waves taking them under. It was commonplace out here. They didn't know there was a shore just a few yards back, a safe shore to go and rest. I wanted to shout to them and tell them all what was just beyond their sight. I looked out and I saw their faces; I looked into their eyes. I could see their skin—every race, every kind, everyone. I could see their eyelashes wet with seawater. I could see their wrinkled fingertips as they raised them above the water. They were all fully dressed as if they had no original intentions of being out here. I could see the desperation in them. They clawed at the top of the water as if it was solid and they might be able to lift themselves out. I started to cry. Then those tears turned to sobbing for them. My breathing was erratic and my heart was beating in my ears. My chest raised up and down faster than it ever had before, but I couldn't catch my breath. I knew just then that they needed saved. I knew the Lord could do that. I turned to Him, I tugged on His hand and, desperate for Him to grab them and make them come back, I said, "Grab them Lord! Save them!" Without speaking out-loud, I heard Him tell me that He wouldn't do that. He made them free to make their own choices. He could call and whisper promises to them, but He would never make that choice for them. I was sobbing now; so uncontrollably my body was shaking. I was safe in my Savior's arms, but there were so many people that were not. I was overcome with desperation for these people.

Just then, I noticed someone in the distance enjoying this scene. He was laughing at these people. I heard him telling the ones at the shore that it was nice out here. Nice out here? What! He was trying to persuade them to come on out. My eyes darted back and forth over the waters, watching him call out to them and seeing their choice. I wanted to run to them to tell them no! The Lord held my hand tighter just as I started to take off; He obviously knew my thoughts. I was standing in disbelief. How could this person be so good that he persuaded all these people to do such a thing and come out here? What was he saying to them? Couldn't they see all the others out here barely hanging onto life? The answer was no, they couldn't see us. I just knew he had blocked their view of reality. As he pulled them out farther, they began to understand the choice they had made was leading to certain death, but they didn't know how to get back. They were not brave enough to swim the distance. They didn't know the power that they held inside. At this point, all their strength was gone. The Lord yelled out to them and held out His hand. Some grabbed it immediately and some swam farther away from Him. They were angry at Him; I could see it. They were mad that He did not save their loved ones from death, angry in their thinking that He caused their terrible circumstance, and angry that their life was painful. They wanted nothing to do with this Jesus and they were staying out here whether that meant death or not. We stood there a little while longer while some people swam to His hands spread wide open. They clung to Him like they would never again let go. Some He called out for a few more times. He spoke louder to some of them. Some He had to go to because they didn't have the strength to come to Him. The ones here were all crying with joy beside me, but the others were still trying to weather the sea on their own.

The Lord looked out in the distance. *These are my loves. These are all the people I died to save. Look at them. Look at them!* In this instant, inside this moment with the Lord, my life changed. I would never again be the same person I was before this moment in time. I would never again be able to cruise through life in a "mediocre Christian" way. I would never again be a coward to spreading the truth of Jesus Christ. I would never again be able to live silently with Jesus walking behind me. I would never again be able to look at hurting people the same way that I always had. In the next instant I stepped over the line between believing in Jesus and following Him. I finally knew who I was created to be. I knew why I was here. My back straightened, my shoulders broadened, and I tightened my grip on His hand. As long as He was with me, I could not fail. The hairs stood up on my neck. I had always proudly told everyone I was part of the body of Christ, but now I knew exactly what I was saying.

I squeezed His hand and looked up into His eyes. I saw the tears streaming down His face at the recognition that some of His children would never grab His hand. His tears followed behind one another in a steady flow down His cheeks. I watched Him watch the people out there. His eyes were that of a parent, desperately asking their child to make the choice to just come home. His eyes were pleading with them. I could feel His body wanted so badly to run out and grab them, but He knew they wouldn't stay if He made them do it. He didn't want much at all. He only wanted them to see how much He loved them. Love, that is all He wanted them to see, nothing more and nothing less. His tears were hitting the water at His waist never to be seen again. I could feel His heart breaking as I held His hand and looked up into His eyes. I felt the urge to look away because His breaking heart crushed my own. I could feel His whole body was broken for His children. My heart was crushed for Him who died on a cross for a world full of people who hated Him, yet didn't ever really know Him. He was crying these tears of sorrow for the angry ones that turned away from Him, for the ones that just walked a few feet away and were taken under. He was crying for the ones that had taken His hand and fallen into the lies from the enemy. And now, here they were. He saw the ones that were swimming from a life of sadness and felt He was the creator of that sadness. Some were out here rebelling against Him. I could see that some, in their grief, wanted nothing to do with Him. Some were swimming away from what they had done and would swim on and on just to try to get away from the guilt. It would forever follow them like an angry shadow. But His death had covered all that they had ever done. His hand could bring them back.

I was angry at that person out there telling them all these lies. I wanted to scream the truth! I was desperate for them to *know my* Jesus, not the Jesus they met from a slew of religious hypocrites, not the Jesus that they thought would make them do this life alone, not the Jesus that they believed created all this pain, and not the Jesus that their enemy told them He was. I was sobbing. My body was racked with sadness. I wanted to tell them how much they were loved! I wanted to tell them what they held inside of them as a child of God. They could get back! They could overcome! They could be victorious!

The Lord turned around to bring us all back to shore. I had seen enough. The sand became softer and the wind died down. The sun started to shine as I stepped onto the beach. As I stood there, I turned around to see where I had come from. I could no longer see all those people flailing. I couldn't even see the ones that had just waded out. Someone was blocking my view. I could hear him lying to me telling me there was no one drowning. I could feel how much he wanted me to come out there alone. His words were deception, all of them. He was telling me everyone was fine and that I should just keep to what I could see. He was even trying to entice me to wade out just a little bit without the One I came with. Enough! I had seen the ugly truth. I wasn't going to rest on this beach until I told as many people as I could that Jesus is the only freedom from the raging sea ahead of them. The only way to overcome the waves is by holding onto the hand of the One who died for them and for us all. He made us to be brave enough to hold onto His hand no matter the waves, strong enough to trust Him in the midst of pummeling waves, and kind enough to reach out a lifesaving hand to the overwhelmed person beside them.

The Aftermath

I want you to meet this Jesus, the real Jesus that loves you more than life itself, the Jesus that will at some point ask you to understand who He is. He wants you to know who it is that you serve. I want you to desire to know Him. Literally, I want your desire to know Him to be so sweltering, burning hot inside you that you will stop at nothing to find out who He is. You are a child of God, *transformed* by what He has done in you! I want you to live that life. I want you to know that you are so very loved! "For God so loved the world that he gave his one and only Son, that whoever believes in him shall not perish but have eternal life" (John 3:16). I want you to know that He chose you. "But we ought always to thank God for you, brothers and sisters loved by the Lord, because God chose you as first fruits to be saved through the sanctifying work of the Spirit and through belief in the truth" (2 Thessalonians 2:13). He hung on the cross, dying for *your* sins, sins that should have meant death for you. But He gave *you* life. "For the wages of sin is death, but the gift of God is eternal life in Christ Jesus our Lord" (Romans 6:23). Your life was meant to be lived holding the hand of Jesus. "So do not fear, for I am with you; do not be dismayed, for I am your God. I will strengthen you and help you; I will uphold you with my righteous right hand" (Isaiah 41:10). I want you to have a life with supernatural meaning. I want you to know how to hold the hand of Jesus and walk closely with Him. I want you to live with the bravery that you are able to do anything that the Lord could ever ask of you. I want you to see that you can walk through the biggest wave of your life and come out unharmed, but only by holding His hand through it. I want you to see that you are not created to be swimming out there all alone. I want you to put your hand in His and then let Him tell you who you are and what you can really do.

I Am Brave. I Am Strong. I Am Kind.

I have heard him utter these words to me when I desperately needed them. *You are brave.* "Be strong and courageous. Do not be afraid or terrified because of them, for the Lord your God goes with you; he will never leave you nor forsake you" (Deuteronomy 31:6), in the midst of tremendous fear, fear of not raising my kids "right," fear of not pleasing everyone, fear of not making the right choice, and fear that my situation would never end. I have heard Him say, *you are strong.* "Have I not commanded you? Be strong and courageous. Do not be afraid; do not be discouraged, for the Lord your God will be with you wherever you go" (Joshua 1:9). I heard this when I thought leaving this earth was my best choice, when I wanted to turn around on this road He was leading me down, when I had to walk away from people I cared for, and when I had to stand up for His ways in my life.

He told me, *you are kind.* "Be kind to one another, tender-hearted, forgiving one another, as God in Christ forgave you" (Ephesians 4:32). I heard this when I stood guilty after spewing hurtful words, when the last thing I wanted to do was forgive, and when I stood self-righteously, spreading judgment. That ever-present small voice of the Holy Spirit told me I was worth it, I was loved, and I had an obligation to show that love. I want you to feel this power, His power, the power that shows us that even though we are sinners, He loves us enough to die for us. "But God demonstrates his own love for us in this: While we were still sinners, Christ died for us" (Romans 5:8). He died for *you* to not only give you heaven but to free you from this life lived in chains. Your enemy will stop at nothing to convince you that the love that was shown to you on Calvary might be enough to take you to heaven, but is definitely not enough to allow you to live life joyous, hopeful, and free.

The War and Your Enemy

You are in a war over what God wants for your life and what the enemy tells you that you want for your life. This is also the same war in which you have to rise up and fight. You have to know your *real* enemy. You are being lied to by a very cunning, very sly liar. "You belong to your father, the devil, and you want to carry out your father's desires. He was a murderer from the beginning, not holding to the truth, for there is no truth in him. When he lies, he speaks his native language, for he is a liar and the father of lies" (John 8:44). He wants to take you down. "Be alert and of sober mind. Your enemy the devil prowls around like a roaring lion looking for someone to devour" (1 Peter 5:8). Satan exists just as much as what you actually see around you and we as Christians either give him too much power or like me before the dream; we do not acknowledge his lies in our lives. Let me tell you this: if you listen to the lies forever that he doesn't care about little old you, he will take you down with him. By taking you down, I mean that you will live in defeat, denial, resentment, and lack of forgiveness and joylessness. There is a spiritual war over all of these things and we as the church are in the center of that war! Our enemy directs our attention from fighting against his lies to fighting anything else that we will pay attention to: our family, our friends, our co-workers, the other volunteers at church, our time, our pastor, our kids, and our addictions. If he keeps you and I always engaged in fighting something other than himself, we will never fight him. We will never turn our swords on the real enemy. "For our struggle is not against flesh and blood, but against the rulers, against the authorities, against the powers of this dark world and against the spiritual forces of evil in the heavenly realms" (Ephesians 6:12). Our enemy was created by God to be an angel of good, "You were anointed as a guardian cherub, for so I ordained you. You were on the holy mount of God; you walked among the fiery stones. You were blameless in your ways from the day you were created till wickedness was found in you" (Ezekiel 28:14–15). He was handed the freedom to choose good or evil and then given in to his own pride; he was cast out of heaven. "And he said to them, 'I saw Satan fall like lightning from heaven'" (Luke 10:18).

His goal is to make you hand over your power that the Lord gave to you so he can use it against you. His schemes are powerful enough to make your heart turn from God. His lies are big enough to make you believe something about yourself that was never true. He wants to make sure you never take the hand of the Lord, and when you do, he will live to make sure you drop it and resent your Creator from that moment on. He wants to make sure you stay out in that violent water all your days here on earth. He will tell you how much you don't need a Savior even after you turn your life over to Him. He will tell you that you are doing just fine on your own. He will make you believe that if you are out there in that water, the Lord has left you, all the while the truth is that the Lord is standing right there next to you. He will tell you that you are the only one in charge of your life. He will tell you that you can keep one foot in the world and one following Him. He will slowly fade you from an on-fire for Christ follower to a person that does not even resemble the former. He lives to make the Lord look bad. He will make you believe the Lord created all the awful things around you. He will make you believe that a Lord that loves you would never allow you to go through what you are going through. He will make you believe that if the Lord loved you so much, He would stop the situation at hand or He would've stopped what happened years ago. He lives to defeat you. He lives to tear you from God. That is your enemy. There are no words to adequately tell you how much I long for you to start fighting your enemy and know the truth about who you are, who you can be, and who the Lord wants you to be. This battle leads you out into dark waters; this is real. And it is war.

The Call

I did not sugarcoat these topics so they look pretty while hollow in the core. I will not tell you anywhere in this book that tomorrow your life will turn around because, circumstantially, it might not. I will not tell you that you will not suffer. What I will tell you is that even if all of life hits you like a truck, you serve a God that will *never leave you*. I want us, as His children, to know who we are in Christ. I want us to live as though we have been freed by Christ and not live as chained-down children of God. I do not want us any longer chained down by what people have told us do with our lives. I do not want us to live chained down by past failures and regrets, chained down by the definition of religion, chained down by the fear we might fail, chained down by missed opportunities, chained down by our lack of strength to take a step, chained down by secrets we have kept for so long, and chained down by a constant uphill struggle. We have to realize these chains before we can begin to ask the Lord to help us break them. I hope through these words and the word of God, we can start to see the chains that keep us from living a victorious life. All these chains I talk about, these were my chains too. My freedom came when I saw the selfless love that He had for me. He broke my chains when I realized just how much it is that He loves me. When I stood out in that water, I saw just how much He loves each and every one of us. There is not one that He did not die to save. I refuse to live anymore like I have not been redeemed and freed by that love.

Faith in a Watered-Down God

We, as born-again believers, have hearts so ransacked by lies from the enemy that we have forgotten where our true identity lies. We have forgotten or perhaps never known the power that we hold with the Spirit living in us! Many of us are flailing through our busy lives and we go to meet Jesus at church on Sundays. We have too many fluffy versions of a God who exists to make us happy. I know these issues are very real. These issues are the very reason people walk around with a smiling face "serving" God, while miserable and heartbroken. These issues are the reason people do not stand up to fight their enemy and take hold of the power of Jesus! These topics will determine if we just like telling people we love Jesus, or we are followers of Jesus whose actions and words prove to people that we love Him. These topics will make us ask ourselves who we really are. These topics will make us get off the fence and go live of the world or take the hand of Jesus, because we *cannot* have it both ways. "Do not love the world or anything in the world. If anyone loves the world, love for the Father is not in them" (1 John 2:15).

Maybe if we got a little uncomfortable sometimes, we would be able to take the first step of change. I was more uncomfortable standing in that murky, raging water than I have *ever* been in my life. I wanted to get out and run to the shore. If it wasn't for that moment, you wouldn't be reading this right now. I want you to be uncomfortable. I want you to look in the mirror and take a good look at *yourself,* and stop weighing your faults with everyone else's. I want some of these topics to be hard for you. Actually, some of these were very difficult for me to write. I want to write about the feel-good parts of following Jesus. But that's not reality and those words will not bring people out of the depths or off the ledges. I want these pages to be soaked with tears and smeared highlighter. I want this book to be a constant reminder of the things that you are, the things that lay inside all of us as children of God. These things need to be prayed about, stewed over, and talked about with friends. They need to sink deep in your soul so you carry them all the days of your life, each and every single day of your life.

My Brokenness

I am literally heart broken. I sit here in the coffee shop seeing all these people pass by me. I see the hurt in their eyes that I never saw before. I see it in the way their shoulders hunch over and look like they just want to rest. I was too busy to see and much too busy to stop and help before my heart was broken. There are so many walking around in the waves, pummeled every single day, and no one can see their hurt. Knowledge of that hurt keeps my fingers going throughout the night when I really need to sleep. If you may be thinking that this is just a book that I wrote in my free time to make a buck, you need to speak with my husband, mother, and grandmother. They will tell you the hurt and desperation I feel in my heart for you. My husband will tell you all the times I sit at the dinner table and cry tears for all the people I see in chains every day. My mother would tell you she wiped tears from my eyes when talking about you in the car driving home, yes, you. My grandmother, if she were here, would tell you how "passionate" doesn't even begin to describe how I feel about my call to help you live in truth and freedom. Some of you are people I have met and I saw your hurt before we even said hello. Most are people I have never met in my life, yet the Lord showed me your hurt. I can write this book because we share the same hurt. We are told the same lies. We share the same truths. We share the same Savior.

Even as a follower of Christ like you, I have been in the deepest valley and the tallest mountaintop. He has brought me from a very deep pit. While down there, the enemy stole my ladder and lied to me about who I was. I know I am not the only one who has felt this deception from the enemy, although he would lead us all to believe that we are alone in our hurt and our circumstances. I want to equip you to be able to know who you are and destroy all the lies from your enemy. I am desperate for the Lord to show you His truth and unlock who you were created to be. Enough is enough! I hear people so hurt and angry and they have no idea how to get free. They carry around all this baggage that they don't even know it is on their shoulders. They've listened to the lies about themselves and God for so long that they accept them as truth. I talk to so many followers every day that cannot hear the voice of the enemy lying to them. He lies to everyone. He tries to chain everyone, even the "seasoned Christians."

I couldn't care less if you have been to church for sixty years. I don't care if you knew the Lord and walked away. I don't care if you define yourself by a denomination or don't. These words are for every person on the planet that say they love Jesus. They are for every walk of life. They are for every follower that has ever been hurt, or lied to, or had something taken from them. It doesn't matter to me who people think you are or who you think you are; let the Lord tell you who you really are in Him. Let Him teach you that you are brave, strong, and kind. Let Him show you how to be victorious! Let's break the chains that are keeping you from living the life you should be living serving Him. Let's break the chains that keep you from rising up to take hold of the hand of God. Let's break the chains that keep you from acknowledging the everlasting love that was shown to you by way of the cross. Let's break the chains that keep you from being who you were created to be. It's time.

Section 1

Brave: Ready to Face Danger or Pain, Showing Courage

Chapter 1

I Am Brave Enough to Accept and Walk in His Truth

I REMEMBER IT WELL WHEN I first accepted the Lord's truth as truth in my life and admitted that I believed that He died for me. I saw His truth. I accepted His truths and knew that He had already accepted me into His family, before I even knew who He was. I was such a young kid. I felt no pressure to do anything from my family or otherwise. I do not even remember looking around to see if anyone else was making this choice like I was. I knew this was my choice and mine alone. No one else could walk this with me. No one else could feel what I felt in my heart. I remember the teacher at my Vacation Bible School telling me the story of Jesus, the story of how He was born and lived a life of no wrong and how He died on a cross. He was buried in a tomb and then arose three days later and is alive today and living in heaven. My heart was telling me that Jesus died for me so I could be with Him someday in heaven. He died to make me righteous and forgive my sins. He chose me without me even choosing Him first. Without Him, I was just a sinner, alone in the world. He loved me enough to die for me. Me? But I thought He didn't even know me. The truth was He did know me. And He chose me. My heart was melting. It was telling me that He was my Savior. It was telling me that what the Bible said was true. Up until now, these were stories I heard in children's church. But something was different now. These stories were somehow making their way to my soul. My heart was telling me even though I was so young, He loved me enough to die for me. Someone died for me. That's hard for anyone to grasp. He literally died on a cross for me. I told my teacher that I felt like I wanted to follow Jesus. I wanted to follow Him forever. She smiled at me. She hugged me. It was a big bear hug like she knew me. She took my hand and led me to a lady older than I had ever seen before.

She was sitting alone in a pew that was covered with scratchy red fabric. An old lady with gray hair and a big fluffy skirt led me to the Lord that day. I will never forget the wrinkles on her hands or how soft they were when she held mine. I will never forget the way her embrace felt when she hugged me. You know the kind of embrace you get from a stranger? Awkward. But not this hug. Her hug told me she loved me and she didn't even know me. I could feel it. I can't tell you exactly what church I attended that day, but I will never forget who the Lord put on my path to guide me. I don't even know her name. She sat and prayed and cried with me. At the time, I didn't understand why she was crying. They were very soft tears, slowly making their way down her cheeks. I couldn't grasp what about a stranger making this choice would make her so upset. She was working for the Lord that day, and every day of her life had led her there to that moment with me. Grasp that. She made a choice that morning to get up and serve the Lord and she sat beside me helping me take that first brave step. The Lord made this moment possible. I am sure there were extremely hard times in her life when she could have walked away from God, but here she sat, helping me to understand Jesus's truth and what it meant to follow Him. When I admitted to her that, yes, I believed that Jesus died for me, I cried just a few tears. I had decided to love and follow Jesus, and my soul knew how monumental that moment was.

The Significance of the Cross for My Life

One day, a good friend and I were chattering about our lives over coffee. We were speaking about how to interact with another woman in a positive way as she tried her patience most of the time. Without even thinking about what she was saying I said, "Well, I guess you're going to have to pray about it." She looked at me blankly and said, "That's so 'generic Christian' of you. Why would I pray about that? I know what He would tell me. He would tell me to just love her. I know Him. He told people to love more than anything else. I will have to just love her. But, I will need to pray about the best way to do that for her." I sat back in amazement. This woman was a prayer warrior. She was in constant prayer all the time, so for her to say she didn't need to pray about this shocked me. It seemed so simple but yet so profound at the same time. She really *knew* her Father. She knew what He would tell her about this just by knowing what He said about it before now. Every verse in her Bible was living to her. She knew He didn't just prompt those that wrote it to write dead words that hold no application to people's lives in this future. Every single written word lived on and nourished the souls of those that read it. She allowed her wisdom of the Lord to direct her actions with every move she made. From that moment on, I wanted to know Him like that. I wanted to know His words that well. I wanted to know His life so well that in some instances, I would know what He commands of me without having to ask.

Even after I had made the decision to find out just who Jesus was, it took me a long time to fully immerse myself in who He was while He was on this earth. I knew well who He was when He bled and died on Calvary. I knew who He was when He arose three days later. I know who He is sitting at the right hand of God. But who was He while walking this earth just like me? I looked at the things that He did, the things that He said and the way that He communicated with His Father. I wanted to *know* Him. I wanted to know just who it was that I said that I served. How could I possibly follow someone that I know next to nothing about? How could I tell others the majesty of who He is if I don't know? What would it look like if I really knew who He was? In turn, what would it look like if I could lead people to Jesus not solely by things that I said but by imitating His actions because I know them so well? What would it look like if I could tell hurting people exactly how Jesus could help them without having to "look it up"?

When Jesus came to this earth as a human, He was fully human but was also fully God. "The Word became flesh and made His dwelling among us. We have seen his glory, the glory of the one and only Son, who came from the Father, full of grace and truth" (John 1:14). Since Jesus was human and therefore had a human mind, He was just as tempted as you and I and yet He never sinned. He spoke to so many about what He commands, the way to follow Him and the way to lead others to Him. He led so many. He performed miracle after miracle on this earth. He equipped people to walk this life with Him holding their hand. Before He was crucified, the authorities in that time looked for reasons to charge Him because He said He was the Son of God. This was blasphemy to them, lies, all lies, even after they witnessed all of the miracles He had performed, lies. Right before He carried His own cross to die, they spit on Him and slapped Him. He remained silent. People that He had handpicked to walk with Him disowned Him, people that had walked with Him His whole adult life, His friends, His comrades. They said they didn't even know Him. He was silent. An enormous crowd of people screamed to crucify Him instead of a known murderer. He didn't say a word. They had Him flogged, whipping Him violently. He didn't say anything. He knew why He was doing this. He was doing it for you and me. They stripped Him and put a scarlet robe on Him. They put a crown of thorns on His head. They spit on Him and hit Him in the head with a staff, over and over and over. They made Him carry His own cross up to the hill where He was to be crucified. They hammered nails into his flesh and onto the cross. They mocked Him while on the cross. "He saved others, they said, but He can't save himself..." (Matthew 27:42).

Actually, He *could* save Himself, but He knew what He had to do. He knew what He was dying for. He *chose* to hang there. Have you processed that? He knew that without His blood being shed, all of humanity would never be released from the chains of their sins. We would never be justified or righteous in Gods eyes. Our spirits would remain dead in sin. We would forever be condemned for the sin that is in us. Our sins could never have been forgiven. We could never have victory in this life. We could never live free. We could never know God. We would have to pay the price for our sins. That price is eternal death, separated from God; that place is Hell. Jesus hung on a cross, blameless, so that His blood would cover all of our wrong. Everything that we have ever done was covered that day on the cross when someone chose to die for us, simply because He loves us. "Greater love has no one than this: to lay down one's life for one's friends" (John 15:13). He went through all of this so that we could know perfect love and be saved, saved from a life without hope, saved from a life of lies, saved from a life without love, and saved from the enemy's grip. The cross means we are free, freedom that was bought and paid for. Someone paid a price for our freedom. Someone died a very brutal death so that we would know perfect love, a love that we do not deserve and forgiveness that we do not deserve. He did all He did and lived as He lived to give us an example to follow. He said the things that He said so that we would know how to speak. He forgave so that we would know how to forgive. Above all, He loved so that we would know love and how to love without asking first when to do it. "We love because He first loved us" (1 John 4:19).

Changing Our Hearts

Sometimes, when we sit in church for years and years, the sacrifice that Jesus made for us dwindles to become just the story we hear before Easter. It becomes just "what He did for us" and not something that causes us to die to our selfish ways and truly follow Him. It becomes a side note, a good story. Sometimes, His death for us solely becomes a fact that we admit when we choose to follow Him. Sometimes, we slowly fade from people that fell at His feet and cried out to Him at our moment of transformation, to people that nod our heads in agreement when we listen to the passages about His crucifixion. We nod now. I nod. You might nod at His brutal death for us. Must we hear the story over and over for it to really "sink in"? Must we watch it on a movie screen with every special effect known to man to really get the "feel" for what it really was? Sometimes, yes. Sometimes our world makes His death fade into just a story we hear on the holidays. Sometimes, we need to hear it again and again so the choice that He made for us never becomes an afterthought. When we become followers of Jesus who are fully aware of what He did for us, we become so grateful to Him that our lives begin to display that gratitude with every step we take.

I know, I know. You, just like I, have accepted that He died for you. I lived just on this level for a long, long time. But I am not talking about just accepting that He died for you. You have already done that. I am talking about accepting that He *chose* to do this for you so that you wouldn't be condemned forever. I am talking about letting that fact change how you view what you are supposed to be doing on this earth. I am talking about a gratefulness so consuming in your heart that everything you do is because of it. He died so you could live, and live you should, holding His hand. Child of God, how much you are loved that He chose a cross in return for you!

Realizing the truth about what Christ did on the cross for you should be life changing. It should be monumental. It should be amazing. Accepting all of what He did for you changes your whole being. It should change the way you walk. It should change the way you talk. It should change the way you live. It should change how you forgive others. It should change the way you love. It does change who you are on the inside. The very definition of you is changed because someone *chose* to show you grace. Is that love or is that love? What would it look like if we lived like this freedom we have was not debt-free. Because it wasn't. You have the bravery inside of you to live every day like your life costed someone their own!

"Yeah, I know. I've been going to church for thirty years. I know the story." *But do you live like you know the cost?* Jesus did not only die to be able to spend eternity with us but also to make us victorious and peaceful in our lives until then! He gave us His Holy Spirit to guide us and direct us every second of every day. As born-again children of God, we possess what others do not. The Holy Spirit lives in us to guide us and speak to us. He exists to help us. He exists to help us to live *knowing* Jesus, not to live only knowing the story. He tries to show us His truths and directs us to walk in that way. We are not supposed to live defeated, resentful, angry, or flailing. He came to this earth to conquer all of those things. He came to this earth and defeated all of the things that chain you down. Did you hear that? He has already defeated all the things that are chaining you down. You just have to make the choice to surrender to God. That surrender means that you die to you, your dreams, your wants, and your selfish choices. You make the choice that you will make steps toward God to have Him rid you of your chains and allow you to live in freedom. You have to decide that you are not holding onto these things any longer. You have to make the choice that you refuse to carry these things on your own back anymore. You have to think of what things are holding you down. What are the things that are there in your life that you feel convicted about when you sit in church? What is it that is making you swim farther away from Him in that water? Is it pain, anger, hurt, lack of forgiveness, or sickness that keeps you from coming to God? Whatever it is, you have to think of it, acknowledge it is keeping you from God, and bring it and yourself to Him. Bring it to Him. Tell Him what it is and what it has done to your relationship. And then lay it at His feet. Give your sorrow to Him and begin to work it out with Him. Whatever it is, His cross has conquered it all. You were not made to carry all of this. He will carry it. He carried it to Calvary and conquered it. You were not made to spend all of your days out in that water. You were made to be holding the hand of Jesus, relying on His strength to conquer your enemy, fears, and pain. I know that chains feel like comfort after many years, but do not be fooled: the comfort you feel in your chains is just that, comfort. It is not peace or joy or hope. Those things exist outside of your comfort and He wants to lead you through change to get to them. You are brave enough to follow Him. Yes, you are.

Weapons for War

We have tools given to us to be able to defend against this enemy and to be able to walk with the Lord through change. This is the armor of God. "Finally, be strong in the Lord and in His mighty power. Put on the full armor of God, so that you can take your stand against the devil's schemes" (Ephesians 6:10–11). Listen, like you, I have heard this "armor" thing so many times coming from the pulpit. Sounds like an interesting thought this armor stuff, huh? It will always be something that we just hear about until the moment that we actually pick up those weapons to use, every day. It will always be just "something interesting" in the Bible until the day you actual have to fight for your peace, until your enemy kicks you while you're down with depression and anxiety, until he convinces you to fight with family members that were given to you to hold you up and help you, until you look up one day and realize the enemy has dragged you out in a tumultuous sea, until your mind is all that controls you, until your enemy is all that you can hear, and until your addiction has eaten away at everything and every relationship you have been given. It will always be just something you have heard about, until? After that "until now" moment, that armor, the gear that the Lord *gives* you to fight your enemy, it becomes real. It becomes something that you have to use every single day. It becomes something you cannot live without. It becomes what you grab every day to survive in this world.

This full head-to-toe armor to defend ourselves is given to us by God. You do not have to ask for it; it is in your possession as His child. If you are like me, you wake up each morning and leave it hanging in your spiritual arsenal, untouched and dusty. My spiritual life changed when I visually saw myself put on the armor that is given to me. I start with my belt. The belt of truth is my foundation for all the other armor. It holds every other piece in place. I know the Lord's truths. I have them in my heart and say them with my mouth. His truth in His word is the foundation for my faith. I know who He is and who I am in Him; I am His child and He is my Father and I am greatly loved. The breastplate of righteousness, the next piece of armor, is a tough one for me. I want to be righteous and obey God, but sometimes it's hard. The enemy lies to me and tells me how I cannot possibly do what the Lord is asking me to do. He tells me that I won't be able to do what the Lord says I will do. Then I have to remember to put on my breastplate to ward off the lies from the enemy when doing what God commands of me. My enemy will attack from all sides and I have to know the Lord's truth to deflect the enemy's blows. My feet are next fitted with the *readiness* that comes from the gospel of peace. Honestly, my feet are not always fitted too tightly with the readiness to spread the gospel. That "good news" that I will be sharing is hidden as truth in my heart but if my feet are not shod with the readiness to spread it, how would I ever move? If I am going to go to the ends of the earth to spread the gospel of peace, I can only do that with the readiness that should be shod on my feet. My own shield of faith cannot just be on my arm forever, it has to be held up. My faith is irrefutable truth. I will not doubt who God is or the fact that He has good plans for me. If I doubt any of that I am lowering my shield of faith and unable to deflect the enemies lies. My shield of faith is sometimes also used for others when they have no faith. I give them my shield. I make my faith known to them. I tell them my trust and faith in Him and hold up my shield for them while they cannot hold up their own. Someone else told me of their faith once and made it tangible to me. They held up their shield for me when my faith was dim. The helmet of salvation? I use it when the enemy lies to me and tells me that I am not good enough to be saved by God's grace. The enemy has arrows of lies meant for me and only my helmet of salvation can keep those away. That sword of truth He gave me? I use it every single day to slice through all the toxic lies the enemy puts in my head. I use it when he tells me to fight with my family. I use it when he tells me lies about someone that is only trying to help me. I use it when he tells me lies about myself and who I am! I use it when someone needs a lifesaving ring while out in that sea and His truths in my words have to defeat the lies that they are hearing. I use it when I feel my flesh desiring to pick up my old addiction to cigarettes again. I use it on myself when I want to dwell in my self-righteous fantasy land. I use it to slice off the hardness around my own heart from time to time when I need it. I literally see myself saying God's word out loud and yielding my sword against the enemy. "For the word of God is alive and active. Shaper than any double-edged sword, it penetrates even to dividing soul and spirit, joints and marrow; it judges the thoughts and attitudes of the heart" (Hebrews 4:12). You, just like me, have to get used to putting on and using this armor. It was not given to us to sit idly by on the shelf while we try desperately by ourselves to fight off things we have no business fighting off alone.

Your enemy is smart with his lies. And until you see him and the lies for what they are, you will never be able to rise up and out of that water. Learn to see his scheming at work in your life and the lives of others! Use the armor He gave you. Raise you head up above the water, see the Lord calling you back with truth, put on your armor, and be brave enough to swim back to Him! You have the bravery to be able to live in the truth that you are equipped to do this life! You have the bravery to be able to fight your enemy. Be brave enough to walk in His truth of the things that you possess as His child! Jesus Himself held the bravery to fight His enemy in the wilderness with God's truth. "Jesus said to him, 'Away from me, Satan! For it is written: Worship the Lord your God, and serve him only'" (Matthew 4:10). We should use His example as we fight the enemy and his lies as well!

Your enemy doesn't want you to live free. He wants you chained forever, swimming out in that sea without the hand of God all the days of your life. See him for who he is! I want you to be free. I want you to choose Jesus, and not just because you want to go to heaven! I want you to choose Him to be your model for bravery. I want you to pick up His hand and let Him lead you! I want you to be delivered from the chains of your pain and circumstance. The Lord is the only one that can deliver you. He is the only one that can bring you back to shore. Let Him bring you back.

His Love Makes Us Content

The enemy once told me the Lord had a lot of rules, rules that would take away the things of the world that I enjoyed. I wanted God's eternal gift but not the rules. I wanted it both ways. I thought I had the best of both worlds. But then, He opened my eyes to the truth. The enemy's blinders came off when I accepted that if He died to free me from sin, it was also me that He promises life to. It was also me that He says He will never leave. It was also me that He walks beside. It was also me that He asks to walk beside Him. It was also me that He asks to leave the world behind. What I failed to see when I thought the Lord has too many rules was how much the Lord really loves me. He loves me enough to make boundaries for me so I don't fall captive to sin. He loves me enough to beckon me to stay close to Him. He loves me enough to surround me with those that can hear Him when I cannot. He loves me enough to correct me when I do not listen to Him. This is His truth for me! He loves me enough to tell me when I walk too far out in that water alone. He loves me enough to teach me His voice so I can decipher it from the voice of the enemy. He loves me enough to hold my hand. He loves me enough to allow me to go through hardships so I take steps closer to Him. He also loves me enough to allow me to be content in Him, pulling me away from all the "happiness" the world wants to offer me.

But, if you are anything like me, when I was hit by a hardship, I recoiled against the Lord because my "happiness" was interrupted. Should I define happiness? A life without sorrow, without hurt, without pain? Happiness was never the goal, but the enemy told me it was. What a lie! How long had I lived trying to be happy? How long have I stayed at my job because "it made me happy"? How long had I never moved from where I was in life because I was happy there? How long had I sat in the same pew, listening to the same sermon, saying "Amen" in the same way but never allowing the Lord to move my heart past stagnant? How long would I have stayed just where I was, doing just what I had always done, just so my "happiness" didn't get interrupted? How long was I going to keep working *for* Jesus but never working *with* Him?

It took me taking a hard look at my life to come to that crossroad of contentment versus happiness. I saw that I was stagnant in Christ because of my desire to remain "happy" on this earth. I took more enjoyment in my worldly possessions and people than I did with following and knowing Christ. My goal for happiness was running the opposite direction of the goal of contentment in Christ.

Now that I have seen that in myself, I desire to follow the Lord in a way that makes me content with what He has given me where I am at right now. I have come to learn that I will not be happy all the time when following Jesus, but I will have peace and joy. I know now that He will ask me to give my money or time to further His kingdom. That, at the beginning, made me uncomfortable and not "happy." Sometimes, His will for me is not what I want! Sometimes, I have to walk through the waves with Him and this does not make me happy, but I am content knowing that He knows what He is doing. I am content knowing that He has a plan. When was the last time you were just content? Content with what you don't have, content with what you do have, and content with what the Lord has for you? Contentment leads to joy. You've seen these people walking around, the weirdos that look joyful even when life is rough. They are the content ones. They might even annoy you. They are the ones whom, no matter what life brings, their hope lies not in things of the world like a job or money or power, but their hope lies in God. They know things on this earth will fail. They know people will fail them, but they know God never will. They are content no matter what God asks of them.

To be truly content, we have to lay it all down. When I say this, I mean that we have to bring all of what we think we need, all of what we think we should be given, all of what we think we deserve, and all of what we have created for ourselves to give it over to God. We relinquish control over our "happiness." We resolve that we are not the ones who will decide what the plan is. But when we do this, we cannot lay down just a little bit of our lives. We cannot say, "Well, God, you can have everything but my job. I want to keep my job. I don't want to move. I don't want to work for you anywhere but here. I want to keep all my money. I want to keep this or that. I don't want to go there or there. I don't want to talk to them or them." If we are really serious about this following Jesus thing, we have to give Him our lives and let Him do whatever He would like with them. We have to be brave enough to lay down our whole life just like Jesus did for us.

I found life and truth the day I realized that He doesn't live to make me happy. The realization hit me like a rock to the head. I was finally done with my "God works for me" mindset and traded it for my "I work for God" mindset. What bravery does it take to walk a path with the Lord in which you can't see the destination? What bravery does it take to follow someone that knows the way but you do not? That bravery that made Moses listen to God and leave his comfort of home to go get His people? That bravery exists in you. That bravery that made Daniel confident in the Lord's promises when he was put in a lion's den? That same bravery is yours. Can you imagine the bravery that Noah possessed when he said yes to building an ark just because the Lord told him to? That bravery is the same bravery that you have inside you! The bravery that made Jesus able to walk His cross to Calvary to die for you? That bravery burns inside of you today. You can go, you can walk, you can listen to God. You can be who He wants you to be and you can do what He asks of you.

He really loves you. His truth is that He will *never* leave you. His truth is that you are created as His child. His truth is life. His truth changes everything. His truth is real. You can quit searching for happiness when these truths hit your soul and dislodge all the enemy's lies about what you deserve in this life. Search for only Him and the peace that He has for you and you will be free to live your life truly holding His hand wherever He leads. You were created to be free and live in truth. You were created to be brave enough to walk anywhere that the Lord will take you, anywhere. His truths for you are all over the Bible. Study them, pray about them, and then live like you are brave enough to be defined by those truths *and* walk in them every single day. "You will seek me and find me when you seek me with all your heart" (Jeremiah 29:13).

Chapter 2

I Am Brave Enough to Accept He Will Change Things

I TOLD THE LORD A long time ago what I wanted to do with my life and asked Him to come along and guide my plan. You know, I wanted to be sure I didn't end up failing. I was asked when I graduated high school: "What do *you* want to do with the rest of your life?" How in the world would I know? I was eighteen years old. I just started being responsible (sometimes) to fill a gas tank two years prior! I was in no place to make a sound decision about the rest of my entire life. Believe me. No one asked me if I had asked the Lord what *He* wanted to do with my life. So, like any good Christian girl would, I prayed for the Lord to help me and I was off! Help me with what? Help me to pay the bill for the college He didn't want me attending in the first place? Help me to pass my tests on the path He didn't want me on to begin with? What was I asking Him for? I didn't really know.

Over the next few years, I was constantly searching. Nothing felt just "right." I tried a few colleges and it never felt right. I was on a road with my own map. I was trying to make my own happiness. After attending a few semesters at different colleges, I chose a new university on my own accord. Although I did feel "happy" where I was at, there was nothing about this time that gave me peace. I was in tears in my apartment when I called my grandma. She immediately knew I was upset. I told her I didn't want to stay, but I didn't want her to be disappointed in me. She was so excited for me to be where I was. She simply asked, "Have you asked the Lord what He wants for you?" I said yes. For the first time in a long time, I had finally asked what He wanted me to do. He didn't want me here. All I felt Him saying was "not be here." I didn't know where to go or what to do, but I knew I couldn't be here. I had to take a step in a different direction. My grandma said she supported me if I knew what He said. She couldn't argue with the Lord.

I came home and went to cosmetology school. Not everyone understood my choice, and to be honest, it was not theirs to understand. I stood firm in that I knew this was where He wanted me. I had prayed about this and asked for His will over my life. I finally felt at peace. How different my walk would have been if I had asked Him to guide my ways from the beginning, before all the semesters at college, the tears and the anguish of feeling lost in the world. If I had only asked Him in the beginning what to do, I would have been doing what He wanted long before this point. But, as it was, I was now doing His will, learning how to stand behind a chair and make people feel amazing.

As I first began to do hair years ago, I realized He had given me a great gift. I had so many relationships with so many women who sat in my chair. What a gift! Most people work around the same people every day, but I did not. Every one of these women was so different. I didn't see the same people even weekly. I watched their lives play out. Their stories were so real. Nothing was sugarcoated when someone sat down to get their hair done. I could minister to them and they ministered to me. I learned so much about human nature and the trials we go through. I learned about decision making. I saw what it really was to walk with Jesus. I saw what it meant to be truly wise. I learned when to stop talking. I learned when my advice was warranted and when it wasn't. I saw them searching for meaning and purpose. I saw strong Christian people falling apart. I saw people on top of the world. I saw deaths, marriages, divorces, loss of children, and pain beyond all understanding. I saw faith big enough to make mountains move and also the bottom of the barrel of hope. I saw Jesus keep His promises and lift them up. I saw some of them take

His hand for the very first time. I saw some of them drop His hand when the enemy told them God wasn't who He said He was after all. I saw them growing. I saw them being disciplined by Him. I saw their hope in God growing. I saw Him changing people, people like you and me.

The Lord placed all of these people in my chair to grow my heart. I can clearly see that now. I was walking in His plan before I even knew there was a plan. He placed these people in my chair to help me as well. I had some pretty dark patches standing behind that chair. But, my clients gave me hope and their faith rocked my world. I wanted to learn from them. I wanted to take in all the good and learn with them from all the bad. I know so many times I missed the things the Lord would have for me because, perhaps, it came from the mouth of someone I didn't think could teach me anything. It may have come from someone that I didn't want to learn something from. I always wanted to listen for the Lord, but I had trouble listening to what He said through others, until I stood behind that chair. Then I saw that I could learn something from everyone. Even if it was what not to do, I could learn. I know it was His plan for me to see so many hurting people sitting in that chair. It was His plan for me to see so many people searching as well. I was desperate for the people in my chair to know Jesus. I was in turn desperate for their families and their coworkers and their church families to see Jesus. I saw their hurt and this brought me face to face with what broke His heart. What was I supposed to do with all this pain that everyone carried around? I wanted the Lord to help them all, but it seemed as though I could do nothing about it!

The First Steps of Change

The winds of change were rolling in. How did I know that? I could just feel it. That's the only thing I can say. I just felt like I was not content anymore. I felt like the Lord wanted to do something with me, but I had no idea what that was. Was it a pull to a new direction, a different step, a new path maybe? I had been working behind the chair for about eight years. I had been moving toward *my* goal of a big hair salon, so I was still taking steps toward that. I had to quit taking new clients because I had all I could take. This was a major accomplishment in my world. Look at what I was accomplishing! Look at all my dreams coming true! Look at me go! I was doing really well. I was on the brink of being all that I wanted to be in the world. I knew what I wanted. Then *my* plan came to a brakes-screeching, losing control, swerving everywhere, fork-in-the-road stop. Remember the winds of change that I spoke about earlier? Yes, those winds had finally blown in.

As I prayed what was going on in my life, the Lord asked me to fast. Now, let's get this straight: I did not grow up around people that fasted for spiritual reasons, nor was I around them now, I presumed. People just didn't talk about those things. I had no idea where to even start. I went to a bookstore and basically read a small book on fasting really quick while I stood in the aisle. I understood what I was about to do and what He was asking me, so I went home and prayed. I told the Lord I loved Him more than anything and I was going to sacrifice some things to know Him more. The next day, I started my fast. I prayed fervently and with passion to Him every single day. I wanted what He wanted for me in a way that I never had before. On day 14 of my 21-day fast, the Lord revealed why I was doing this: He told me He wanted me to write a book. Yes, that's right. He just told me. It was simply that. "I want you to write a book." I heard it in my mind as clear as I would have if someone were standing beside me. Wait, what? Me? Maybe He rang the wrong phone. Maybe the operator from heaven got the lines switched?

Listen, I am busy. (So are you.) I live life. (So do you.) I have a husband. I have a business. I have three kids under eight, and God, you want *me* to write a book? That was my response to *God*. My husband gave me the deer-in-the-headlights look when I told him. He just sat there and blankly stared at me. I knew he believed me, but it was hard to trust what I was saying was really from God. I understood that. I would just have to prove it to Him. The Lord was going to take me somewhere that only He knew that path, a place where He would not tell me everything that was going to happen. In fact,

He was only going to tell me the next step every step of the way. That was it. He literally equipped me for what I needed exactly when I needed it and not a moment before. He chose something that I knew nothing about. I have no experience, no dealings with, or know-how of the writing world. I would have to blindly trust the Lord. I would not be able to lean on anyone else and certainly not myself. For the first time in my life, I was going to have to take His hand and walk with Him when I could not see my next step. It is easy to be brave and step out when you know the road under your feet exists and to where it leads. It is quite a different act of bravery to walk out with Jesus when He doesn't show you the new path or what, if anything, lies beneath your feet.

Trust Is Bravery

I did not leap off my couch to begin this journey. I will be honest, I was more nervous than I had ever been in my life. My life was easy where I was and I was "happy" doing what I was doing. But that was not the goal, and He reminded me of that. When faced with the choice to keep walking on my own road or follow Jesus to a new road, I was overwhelmed. The two roads were just as you can imagine. The one road I could see was very familiar. It was pretty and well lit, but Jesus wasn't leading there anymore. It was everything that I knew. It was a continuation of the path that I had been on for so long now. It was comfortable and easy, and frankly, I knew what I was doing. The other road was not so well lit and looked, let me just say, dark, except for the lamp the Lord possessed. He was there on that side. But there was absolutely nothing about that path that looked familiar except for the Lord. I could only see the beginning stepping stone on that path and nothing more.

How would I decide between these two roads? (One of which wasn't a road at all mind you, merely a path just wide enough for two people. *And* let me remind you, I was *not* a writer.) Now, let me explain this to you. I had been doing what the Lord wanted me to do. He told me. I heard it. But, as I sat there on my couch, it hit me:

I knew that His plan for me all along was to do hair and learn all of what I had and then move on. His plan never changed for me; this move to a new path was part of the plan. I realized in that moment, staring at these options, if I chose to go straight ahead on the road I was on, Jesus was taking a backseat to my mapping skills from here on out. I could stay on the road in which I had worked so hard, or go to the new one with Him. What did I know? Who was I to lead? To where? To hope in myself it would all work out like I had planned? The road I had been on was obviously more comfortable for me. Did I know where that road would take me now? No. Who held the map for that road from here on out? Me. That didn't make me feel confident at all. I did know that He had a plan much bigger than I could ever see. I did know He loved me more than I could even imagine. I knew His plan for me was good. I knew I had to trust that He would be with me and that He would be guiding me. I was also reminded that just because I chose this path, that did not mean it would all be rainbows and sunshine. There would be stumbling blocks, trying times, and tears. I knew it would only make me stronger and bring me closer to Him.

I decided that I didn't want my road anymore. I didn't want my dreams anymore. They didn't look nearly as pretty now as I was convinced they were. I took everything that I had wanted out of this life (and it was a long bucket list) and I bravely laid it all down at the feet of Jesus that day. I remember praying to Him as I was visualizing bringing all my dreams to Him and placing them at His feet. "Here, Lord, I do not want these any longer. I only want for me what you want for me, whatever that is and wherever that takes me." I cried. Satan told me I had worked too hard to give it all up. He said all my work was now for nothing. He said people would laugh at me. He said no one would believe I could do this. He said I would fail. He said my family would think this was stupid because they wouldn't understand. (My family? His lies can't sink too low.) His lies were never ending. He told me that everything I had done standing behind that chair was useless now. Then the Lord reminded me that if I had not gone through and seen and heard what I had, I wouldn't be able to do what I was about to do. All those years of doing what I did had led me to this moment. He was using all of my past to play out His plan. He told me that big bag of my hopes were not His dreams for me. I had worked a long time to aspire to be what I wanted to be. I had to lay it all down. I took His plan for me to do hair and I ran with it. I made it something that it was never supposed to be; I was never supposed to have a big salon like I was planning. I was supposed to be content with what I had and what I was doing. I had the ability to dream big, but I did not make sure those were His dreams for me as well.

Here, I was laying it all down and willing to accept He would change things. I guess this is why He says, "Therefore do not worry about tomorrow, for tomorrow will worry about itself. Each day has enough trouble of its own" (Matthew 6:34). I don't think this means not to plan ahead, but if I had prayed every day just for His will and nothing more, I would have not worried about my dreams of a big salon that would never come to be. I should have told Him the dreams I had for my business and asked Him if He wanted me to proceed with those. I should have asked Him if my goals in life were also His goals for my life. He is my leader, my guide, my Father. I should have treated Him like He was the One leading me, not the other way around.

As I got out of the driver's seat that day and walked over to Him to start this new path, I looked back at all I had done. It was the last time I would look back. I could see that at the beginning, when I came home from school and started to do hair, the Lord's footprints were slightly ahead me, just enough to hold my hand but still close enough for Him to lead me at the same time. When I looked at these last few years, His footprints were behind mine. I was leading Him. Why had I not seen this before now?

I couldn't see it because I didn't want to. The enemy had convinced me that I needed more money, a bigger shop, and a bigger name for myself and I ran with that lie. Now I wanted to see the truth. I never asked for the truth before. As I turned around and grabbed His hand to start this new chapter, I said "Yes, Lord, I will do it. I will go, wherever that is." He looked at me and told me: "For I know the plans I have for you, Kristin, plans to prosper you and not to harm you, plans to give you hope and a future." He smiled at me. There it was, again. His love for me. Those words were now my words to live by. I took the words that He said to me and I memorized them: Jeremiah 29:11. I tell them to myself when I feel doubt creeping in. I tell them to myself when everyone around me says it cannot be done. I bravely trust Jesus. I trust His plans for me. I trust that His plans are bigger than I can see. I trust Him enough to not want to be in control. I trust Him enough to know this path might also change again someday. I am content with where I am right now, not clamoring to see where I will be in five years. I will not get ahead of Him again. I will consult Him in every step. I will ask Him if this is still the path He wants me on. Every day I will ask.

His Guiding Hand

People heard my plan and looked at me, shocked. "Do you know anything about writing a book?" they asked. I told them absolutely not. I had no idea. I didn't know the format, I didn't know how to make an outline, and I didn't know the title or what it was going to be about. I didn't know how to type; I didn't know how long it would take or even how to start. But this I knew for sure: The maker of the stars knew everything about writing a book. He knew what He wanted me to say and how I was supposed to say it, so I wasn't worried about that. He knew people to get this book "out there." He already had them all lined up, so I wasn't worried about that. He knew editors and publishers and people in the industry. I knew that He had told them this was coming. They had prayed for this book too. He weaved our stories together to make this book an answer to their prayers. That's just how amazing He is. He knew all the people who would read this. He knew all the people who He wanted to speak to. He knew *you.* You were a part of this. (And I have prayed for you.) Wrap your brain around that! He loves you that much.

He has already put all the people in place to make this work out according to His will, not mine, whatever His will is and wherever His will would take me. It sounds crazy. It sounds like I'm a nut. I realize this. But if I could tell you everything that He has done so far with this book, you would be astounded! I now know the bravery that I hold inside of me. I know this because He asked me to use it and I did. I had to. I had to bravely go with Him like I had never done before! I had to put my faith into action! Now every time I feel the enemy telling me this will be a flop, that I am a nobody while trying to entice me to go back to my worldly dreams, I squeeze the Lord's hand and remind myself that He knows the plans He has for me. His dreams are now *my* dreams. His heart is now my heart. His fingers are now laced through mine. His plans are now my plans. I am finding my contentment in Him guiding me. He loves me enough to *want* to guide me.

I know it sounds like a perfect thought that He wants to and is able to guide us, but how do we hand over the control of our very own lives? We *follow* Him. We have to take a backseat to His plans. Remember when I looked back at my path with Him and saw my footprints ahead of His? We have to try to not ever let that happen. We have to listen to those that can see it happening to us. If and when we have moved ahead of Him, we have to recognize that move and then fall back into step with Him. In order for Him to guide us, we have to stay in check. We have to pray that we are on the right path all the time. Sometimes, not knowing what lies ahead is the best place to be: it means that you are not the one that is leading.

Don't Forget All He Has Done

Then I sat down and wrote out the whole book and felt wonderful the whole time! I am kidding. That is not how this went at all. In the middle of writing this book, Satan told me I was wrong about all of this. I had a lot written when I felt this defeat. I had worked hard to seek the Lord every single day to know what to write. But who was I to think I could write something like this anyway? I was not a Bible scholar. What if it really was terrible writing? What if I heard Him incorrectly and this was not what He said? What if I really could not do what He was asking? I was defeated. So, I prayed what was a very real prayer, for me, in that very moment, on my knees. "Lord, I am doubting what you have told me. Satan has made me think I am not who you say I am. He's made me think I will not do the things you say I will do. Forgive me for doubting you. I cannot continue with this doubt. This is crippling me. Please, tell me who I really am." I listened for a moment. It was deathly silent in my living room. I was not analyzing my plan. I wasn't arguing with Him about it. I wasn't trying to figure anything out. I just wanted to hear from Him. And then I did. *For I know the plans I have for you Kristin. Plans to prosper you, Kristin. Not to harm you, Kristin. Plans to give you hope and a future, Kristin. I love you.* There it was. His never-ending love for me.

His answer to my prayer that day wasn't long and heavy. It wasn't confusing. It wasn't condemnation for stumbling. It wasn't shame for doubting. I got up and dusted off my knees. Tears fell from my eyes. He loved me. He loved *me*. I was greatly loved. If I could look back and only see Him dying on a cross for me, that was enough to allow me to walk by faith. He cared enough about this small doubt in my life, so I know He cared about my future even when I could not see it.

My faith says even when I cannot see His plans, I know He holds tomorrow and there *is a plan.* I know I will stumble and I know I will fall. If I go through a time when He calls me out into the water during this plan, I will know He knows what He is doing. I will learn and I will be stronger because of the waves. I will not listen to the enemy telling me He has left me. I will grab His hand and not fear tomorrow or the storm. He has declared His plans for me and I am following Him. No enemy is big enough to change that. This book was my proof of that. What is the proof in your life to allow you to walk bravery forward with the Lord? For the first time in your life, let His truth that He loves you and will never leave you be enough for you to move out of comfort. He will change things. He might even change everything. What would life look like if you searched His heart for your plans and quit relying on just doing what you've always done? You are brave enough to ask *His* plans for you and brave enough to follow Him to those plans.

Chapter 3

I Am Brave Enough to Accept He Can Forgive All My Sins

WHEN JESUS DIED ON the cross, He did not put us into categories. "These people I'll shed the most blood for, these people I'll shed just a little blood for; and these people I will only shed a tiny amount of blood for. I hope that covers everyone." Doesn't that just sound absolutely ridiculous? He died the same death for all of us. But if you are anything like me, you might struggle with the reality that Jesus' blood does, in fact, cover everything. The enemy lies to me and tells me that my sins are too bad for the blood of Christ to cover. He tells me that when I do sin, I should be ashamed of myself and live in that shame. He fills my head with so many lies about who I am. Lies like "if you really knew Him, you wouldn't have done that" and "now you don't look like a follower of Jesus" or "He is so ashamed to call you His child now, just stay away from Him." So, sometimes I do just what the enemy tells me to do: I stay away from God. I cower in the corner because of my shame. I avoid praying and seeking Him because of my shame. I pull myself away from God. I start to think that my enemy is right and that maybe I am too bad for forgiveness, especially since I am a follower of Jesus. I start to believe that the sin that I committed is too bad for me to come back to Him.

When I start to feel myself pulling away from Him because of my shame and doubt, it is then that I can feel the Lord calling me back. I can hear Him calling out my name as I start to swim away from Him through the water. I see His hands that are scarred for me and I remember that He died to set me free from my sins. He died so that I could live victorious even though I will sin against Him. He has those holes in His hands to prove to me that He paid the price of guilt and shame so that I would not have to. Even though I know all of this, I will not lie and say it is easy to come back to Him. It is very tough for me to come to Jesus and tell Him the wrong that I have done. It is hard to swallow my pride and to bring my sin to Him and ask for forgiveness. It is difficult to say my sin out loud in front of Him. But when I finally come back to Him and seek His forgiveness, it is then that He can tell me just how much He loves me. He reminds me things like, "For as high as the heavens are above the earth, so great is his love for those who fear him; as far as the east is from the west, so far has he removed our transgressions from us" (Psalm 103:11–12). I can come to Him because I know that He loves me; His death is proof of that. He is my Father and He wants me to bring my sin and shame to Him. He wants me to bravely tell Him what I have done. He wants to show me His love through forgiveness. He does not want me to spend my days in the water on my own because I have too much shame to come to Him. He wants me to be able to hear the lies from the enemy telling me I am too far from forgiveness. He wants to forgive me and pull me from the waters. There is no sin that can separate me from His love. There is nothing that can remove me from His hand. "For I am convinced that neither death nor life, neither angels nor demons, neither the present nor the future, nor any powers, neither height nor depth, nor anything else in all creation, will be able to separate us from the love of God that is in Christ Jesus our Lord" (Romans 8:38–39). This verse is my brave truth when I sin. This verse allows me to come to Him, ask for forgiveness, and walk hand in hand with Him, unashamed, knowing there is nothing that I have done or could do that can separate me from Him.

Seeing My Sin

I have a judgmental attitude sometimes; I will just admit that. I tend to breeze right over my own sin when I am condemning others of their sins. My enemy lives to convince me that my sin is far less than everyone else's so I never deal with my own. He lives to convince me that I should be a lot more worried about others' sins than my own. If I am convinced that my "little" sins are nothing compared to everyone else's "big" sins, why would I ever deal with the sin in my own heart? The truth is I wouldn't deal with it. I would continue to allow my enemy to tell me that I could point fingers of judgment even in the midst of my own sin. By listening to truths from the Lord, truths like "For the wages of sin is death…" (Romans 6:23) and "…for all have sinned and fall short of the glory of God…" (Romans 3:23), I can see that it is not my position to judge another on their sin when all of our sin brings death and separates us from God. I am commanded to love others and to repent of my own sin. I am not commanded to judge others for their sins. I can see clearly what my sin is if I listen to what the Lord tells me. He will search my heart and tell me what I have done that is keeping me from enjoying complete freedom in Him. My enemy wants to sugarcoat my sins so that I never bring them to my Father. On the other hand, my Father wants to tell me what sins I have hidden in my heart so that I can repent and He and I can live and walk together in unity. I always go back to this verse when I am asking the Lord to make my sin known to me so that I can walk with Him, uninhibited: "Search me, God, and know my heart; test me and know my anxious thoughts. See if there is any offensive way in me, and lead me in the way everlasting" (Psalm 139:23–24). It is when I pray this prayer that the Lord shows me what I have in my heart that would inhibit us from walking freely together. It is when I pray this prayer that I am solely thinking about my sin and not fussing over the sins of others. I find that when I begin to worry less about others' sins, I can begin to turn my eyes on my own reflection. This self-reflection leads to the acknowledgment of my own sins and subsequent repentance from myself and forgiveness from my Father. What would the Lord reveal to you if you prayed this prayer? Are you brave enough to ask?

Letting Go

If you are anything like me, you have heard someone tell you to "let it go" numerous times in your life. And if you have a personality anything like mine, you smiled at them and then thought to yourself, "They don't know what I've done. They don't know what was done to me, and if they did, they wouldn't tell me to let it go." But the truth of the matter is that they possibly know something that you do not: they don't need to know what you have done to know that God is bigger than all of it. You can let it go to Him and He is strong enough to take it all. I talk to so many people that are weary and heavy burdened because of the weight of their own sins and the sins of others against them.

If we want to find true inner peace, we cannot carry all our sins around each and every day. It makes us walk around carrying a heavy load. It gives us stress, causing us anxiety and depressing us. Can we even grasp what kind of weight that puts on our shoulders? God did not create us to walk around carrying anything on our shoulders, not sin or regret or defeat or anger or lack of forgiveness. We were made to stand tall, acknowledging that Jesus has taken all of our sin from us. We were created to live in harmony with God, allowing nothing of this world to come between us and Him.

Separation from God Is Not from God

There is nothing that you could've done or said that will separate you from God. There is no sin that He has not conquered. You enemy would want you to live under the weight of your choices your entire existence here on earth. He would want you to live chained down by the choices of others your whole life. He would want you to be chained down by all the things in your past so you never rise and take hold of your Savior's hand. He loves you so much and He made you brave enough to face your sin and turn from it. Get it all out. Let it all go. Sit down with Him. Bring all your baggage from all your life. Tell Him what it is. Tell Him your hurts, your pain, and your sadness. Tell Him your anger and your lack of forgiveness, and then ask if He sees anything else in you that needs sifted out. And when He shows you those things and when you admit them, give them to Him. Take them off your shoulders and give them away. Let Him take them all away. It's time for you to exhibit the bravery that He has given you. Don't keep swimming farther from Him because of the shame of your sin. He sees it. He saw it a long time ago. He just wants it. He wants you to give it to Him so you can live free.

Of all the times I've let you down,
Of all the years I've tried alone.
Of all the lies I told my heart,
In you the only One, I've found.
My sins just seemed too much.
My cries just never stopped.
My mountains raised so tall,
I didn't believe you could take it all.
So broken and sad, I carried it under my smile.
I never forgave, I never forgot,
I never let go and I never stopped.
You told everyone you loved them,
they said it felt so good.
But they don't have a past like mine,
and for that they have misunderstood.
You could never love someone like me,
I figured that out when things kept happening, just to me.
So I kept it in, and sat my pew,
week after week my patience I outgrew.
On my way out, I saw it, the cross.
And there He was, my burdens laying there.
He took all my past and hung there for me.
I saw it.

I felt it.
I finally understood.
I asked Him to take them.
All the feelings I kept in;
Of resentment, and bitterness, and love I've never had.
He's mending those scars,
and it's not overnight.
But, the process I've decided,
is well worth my fight.
So, keep doing this to yourself,
it's not hurting anyone but you.
The fact is, He's worth fighting for,
and He told me that you are, too.

Chapter 4

I Am Brave Enough to Trust Him

MY GRANDPA HAD A certain cow that hated children. She did not mind anyone taller than four feet. She would spot children from the gate and run at us to try to take us down. Venturing into the pasture alone seemed like certain death. I remember a day when I was standing at the gate, overlooking the pasture, wanting to cross the pasture to be with my grandpa in the barn. He must have seen me standing there because he came from the barn to get me to take me back with him. He came close and opened the gate. He motioned me through the gate and stuck out his hand to me. Sheer panic spread through my veins. Did he know what he was doing? Was he aware that she was staring at us right now? I had been watching her for a good fifteen minutes, just as she was also watching me. She pretended the whole time to be eating grass, but I could tell she was most certainly stalking me. He looked down and simply said, "She won't hurt you when you're with me." I wasn't too sure about that.

I saw her walking toward us the second we moved out of the gate. It was like my grandpa didn't even look up to see where she was! I was terrified. He wasn't paying attention! I trusted my grandpa, but that cow was huge! Even though I was holding the hand of my very competent grandfather, I feared that he would not be able to protect me. Even though He was a big man, I was overcome with anxiety that even if he was with me, we would both be taken down!

When we're dealing with a situation that the Lord has brought us to, the enemy will lie to us constantly and tell us that God is not big enough to get us past the situation. We have to ask the Lord to help us be brave. When someone first told me to ask Him for things like bravery, I was perplexed. "Wouldn't He just give me bravery? Aren't I just equipped with it?" Well, yes and no. Yes, we do possess bravery, but sometimes we have to ask for Him to help us use it. Our Father wants to have a relationship with us, a relationship that consists of us talking to Him. He wants to hear from our very own mouths what we need. He wants us to be comfortable coming to Him to ask for everything. I believe this is why the Bible tells us in 1 Thessalonians 5:16–18, "Rejoice always, pray continually, give thanks in all circumstances; for this is God's will for you in Christ Jesus." A good reason that He would want us to pray continually is because the enemy is attacking our walk all the time. I don't know about you, but I want to be ready at all times when the devil comes prowling around. I want the Lord's fingers laced through mine when the enemy comes! Where do you stand and whose hand are you holding to take cover from the giants?

How many times would we love to turn and go back to safety when we see how huge the problem is facing us? How often do we not trust Jesus when He takes our hands to lead us out to the waves? Let's be honest: sometimes it would be so nice to be able to physically see Jesus leading us out into the water. It would be easier to face a giant if we actually felt the Lord's fingers laced through ours. Satan tells us that Jesus isn't with us, that He has left us all alone when we come up against giants. But the truth is that God will "…never leave you nor forsake you." (Deuteronomy 31:6). Hold the Lord's hand every day so that when a giant comes, His hand feels comfortable and you've trusted His guidance way before you have to go out into the waves.

The Lord Can Be Trusted

Once we were a few feet in the gate, the cow started to pick up her pace toward us. She was coming at a pretty good clip now.

"Grandpa," I whispered to him. He just held my hand tighter. In my head, I was having a quick conversation, one that sounded a lot like what I ask myself about the Lord. "Does he not see what's going on here? Is he not even paying attention anymore? Is he going to do anything at all about this problem? Is he even aware of what I am facing?" Sound familiar? That cow got really close before my grandpa said anything. "Hey, hey, hey!" he yelled at her and held up his hand. She stopped dead in her tracks like he had some sort of power over her. She stood and stared at us for what felt like an eternity. She had fury in her eyes. Then she calmly turned around and walked away. I stood shaking down to my core. She knew who the boss was. She knew who held the power in this barn lot. From that moment on, I trusted my grandpa. The rest of the time that I knew him, if he asked me to take his hand and walk with him, wherever we would go, I trusted him. I did not always know where we were going. I did not always know where he was taking me. Wherever we went, we always had to go through the barn lot and that cow was always there watching us. But I never doubted his presence to protect me. I never doubted that my enemy would stop when he raised his hands. Walking with him once through a very scary situation proved to me that he could be trusted. What if I had refused to walk with him? What if I had never just trusted him and walked through the barn lot? What if I had never stared down that giant and looked in her ferocious eyes? Then I would have never relied on someone else's bravery and strength. I would never have known what it meant to trust someone other than myself. I would have never learned to hold someone else's hand and trust they could protect me as they lead me.

But to be truthful, trusting is sometimes difficult, especially when we have trusted people before and then we have been let down. In turn, if we find it very difficult to trust people, then we usually find it difficult to trust God. Luckily, God doesn't operate like people do. He works in completely different ways than people. He knows just how far to stretch your trust. He knows just what lesson to teach and when. When I think back to those moments before walking through the gate with my grandpa, I remember knowing that my grandpa would never let that cow hurt me, but it was still so difficult to take his hand and go out of the gate! However, I knew my grandpa and I trusted how much he loved me. I knew in my heart that he would never do anything that might allow me to be harmed, so I was able to take his hand and walk with him. This was not to say that I wasn't fearful as I walked, but I trusted the person whose hand I held. Isn't this the same way that we should view trust with God? We are human, and therefore, we will feel fear before we trust. But our walk with the Lord is not defined by whether or not we have fear; it is defined by our trust in the Lord to walk through that fear with Him. Sometimes, we can stay forever in the same place because we do not have enough trust in Jesus to move forward. Our fears overcome us sometimes. Trust is hard and trusting someone that we cannot see is even harder. But when we understand the love of Jesus for us by way of the cross, we can begin to understand that He would never die for us, then lead us astray. He died so that He could walk with us and dispel all of our fears. "Peace I leave with you; my peace I give you. I do not give to you as the world gives. Do not let your hearts be troubled and do not be afraid" (John 14:27). Whether we realize it or not, every time God allows a giant to face us, He gives us the opportunity to take His hand and trust Him. The Lord will give us small lessons in trust along our walk with Him so that at some point, we can blindly walk in faith, knowing that He can always be trusted no matter the size of the giant ahead of us. At some point in our walk, we likely won't fear the size of the giant because we know whose hand we hold. We will be able to stand at the gate to the big barn lot and say, "Whom shall I fear?"

Just Keep Walking

I find that often times when being asked to walk out of the gate with the Lord or when He asks me to come out onto the waves, He only asks me to take one step at a time. He has never asked me to take off running with Him. (Not to say He wouldn't, He just has not yet.) He always leads me to just one step, one next move, one next moment of trust. Sometimes, in my walk, I have asked numerous times to just be brave enough to take a step. That is all, just a single step. Matthew 7:7 says, "Ask and it will be given to you; seek and you will find; knock and the door will be opened to you." When we really seek His will, we will find it. When we really ask for the next step He wants us to take, He will lead us. When we really can't see the plan, sometimes, it's best we only take a step at a time. This is why he gives us His word, a lamp, to guide us. "Your word is a lamp for my feet, a light on my path" (Psalm 119:105). How much light does a lamp put off? Just enough to light the space around our feet. This lamp is not a blazing spotlight shining out to light our whole path like we desire it to. It is solely a lamp that illuminates just enough to show us where our next step should be. We think we want to see the whole path, the whole plan, but really, it's too big for us to comprehend.

Most of the time in my own life, He did not show me the whole plan because it would have scared me. He didn't show me the whole path that we would be walking; He only asked me to take His hand most times. If He had shown me where we would be going, it would likely have caused me so much fear that I would never have taken the first step. He wanted to show me how brave I was, but He can only show me that if I walked with Him into the waves. He wanted to show me the bravery that laid inside of me as a child of His. He wanted to show me who He was. He just wanted me to trust Him with every step I took. He wanted me to trust the hand that I held while up against every giant I faced, knowing that I was more than just an overcomer, "No, in all these things we are more than conquerors through Him who loved us" (Romans 8:37).

What giant are you facing that seems absolutely monstrous to you? What would that same giant look like if you looked at it while holding the hand of God and remembered His promises to you? I have found in my own life that when I view my giants standing in front of me, they are always much bigger than myself. They tower above me, they look un-moveable, and they cause me to be fearful. However, when I take the hand of the Lord, my giants don't look near as big as they did before. With His hand in mine, my giants fall at His feet. With His hand in mine, He tells me, "So do not fear, for I am with you; do not be dismayed, for I am your God. I will strengthen you and help you; I will uphold you with my righteous right hand" (Isaiah 41:10). Why do I stand at the gate and fear my giants? Why can I not go out into the waves if He is standing there asking me to? Do you lack the bravery to walk? I assure you, you have the needed bravery inside of you. Wherever you are, He is standing right there asking you to take His hand and walk with Him. He will strengthen you and uphold you; that is a promise. All you have to do is walk, one step at a time. You'd better get going. His plan has been waiting for you.

Chapter 5

I Am Brave Enough to Not Be of the World

(In it, but not of it)

HAVE YOU EVER LOOKED at someone's life from far away and everything looked so perfect? Then the closer you got you realized it was just a mirage? We all fail and we all fall short, but it just doesn't feel that way sometimes. Honestly, it doesn't feel that way almost every single day. We watch "reality TV" and that doesn't look like how we live! We get on social media and our lives don't look like everyone else's. Our lives are messy and wrecked and sometimes we ourselves can't even look! That's reality! We live in a world of corrupt values and humans at odds with God. This is the "world" we live in. This world teaches us that the only way to be happy is to achieve, achieve, achieve! We work tirelessly to achieve to a great position at work. We work to achieve the best house, the nicest clothes, the most friends, and the most talented kids on the team. We work to achieve one worldly prize after another, but do we stop to think about working to attain the prizes that come from walking with the Lord? Do we work to achieve His prize of peace in all we do and say, His love to all, His kindness to the world, His definition of joy, and His contentment? Do we work to spread His gospel? If not, then why are we Christians? Are we just waiting around until we get to go to heaven?

This was me. This was me with one foot in the world and one foot following Jesus.

The Struggle

Trying to live pursing two different things was inadvertently making me become weary and tired. You might also feel yourself being weary and tired of trying to do and have it all. You might feel tired of trying to follow Jesus but also desperately seeking things of the world. He tells us in Matthew 11:28, "Come to me, all you who are weary and burdened, and I will give you rest." He would be the One to give us rest when we are weary and tired, tired of always craving the best of everything and tired of always trying to be better than others and trying to always make it seem like we have it all together. The world makes us search forever for the latest and greatest thing, and when we think we find it, we realize that wasn't that satisfying. We are weary because the world makes us feel defeated and unhappy and always searching. It will suck the life right out of us. It will lure us to places that we never thought we would ever go. If we could ever come to terms with the truth of our lives, we might be able to say that both feet are off chasing the world, and not one foot is following Him.

I struggled with this for so long. I wanted so desperately to walk hand in hand with Jesus, but I had the desire to also live like people of the world, people that were not guided by the Lord and not content with what the He had for them. I wanted to have all the material things that everyone else had. I wanted to do all the things that "successful" people did. I wanted to be "all in" following Jesus, but I wanted all of these other things too. I felt like I was doing everything "right," but something was missing. I couldn't put my finger on it. My life was not giving me the fulfillment I thought it should. My house wasn't making me happy. My job was leaving me always wanting more. I could never make enough money. I would have never admitted it back then, but I was all consumed with worldly prosperity! I worked forty hours a week and my husband did as well. We came home and I slapped dinner on the table. I cleaned up and did laundry and tried to clean and play with the kids. We put the kids to bed, and when we were finally wiped out, we put ourselves to bed. I got to the point that I just knew there was more than this to life. There had to be more to this life than just the same monotony every single day. Was it just me doing something wrong? Was it the wrong church? The wrong pastor? The wrong pew? Was it the people I had surrounded myself with? Was I in the wrong profession?

And then there was a moment of prayer and deep reflection on my part. I was done wandering around. I was done desiring but not really knowing what it was that I desired. I had not been on my knees in quite some time. So, I got down and bowed my head before my Creator. I asked the Lord what it was that I was doing. I told Him I was flailing and never felt like I had a moment to even breathe. I told Him that I didn't think this was how life was supposed to be. I told Him that I felt like I had gotten caught up in my life. I told Him I just felt like I was constantly doing only to really get nothing done. I spoke to Him of desiring to do things that furthered His kingdom; I just didn't know what those "things" were supposed to be. I told Him I loved Him so very much and I wanted my life to show that. I asked Him to take my heart and change it. I wanted my heart to only desire Him. I wanted Him to tell me what He wanted out of me. I was silent after that.

Then it was like my mind opened up and I saw myself going through my life, one thing after another. Memories came flooding through my mind. It was a quick walk through my life. And, it didn't take me long to be able to see through the memories that I was working for the world and not for Christ. I couldn't even tell from my own memories that I myself followed Christ. I could see that I was trying to attain something, but what that was, I couldn't tell. I never attained anything that made me truly happy. Honestly, I had never stopped to ask what it was that the Lord wanted me to be doing. I realized I was so consumed with my own worldly prosperity that I didn't have a second to see myself walking away from my Savior. This is exactly where the enemy wanted me. He wanted me to lead such a busy, crazy life that I didn't have a second to help others walk closer with Christ much less have time to make sure that I was walking closer with Christ myself. As I sat there, recalling all of these memories, all I could see were all the things that I had been chasing, all the hours spent doing nothing that would further His kingdom, all the time wasted for something that would leave me as empty as before. I saw that I had been sucked into a world that gives God no glory, a world where it's every man for himself, a world that taught me that I was the creator of my own destiny. That world made me desire nothing of the kingdom of God, and frankly, the only time I thought of the kingdom of God was on Sundays, during church.

Then one memory stopped it all. My mind slowed as I examined this memory. It was as if a video recorder was on slow motion and I was watching the playback. I saw myself meeting a friend for the first time as volunteers in the church nursery. We would grow to become great friends as we drew each other closer to God. Then I saw myself being asked to baptize her. I could see the two of us standing in the water together. I could see myself asking her some questions about the Lord. I could see her smiling. I could see the joy in her eyes. I could feel the Holy Spirit surround us in that tank. It was just the three of us, never mind the crowd of hundreds watching. It was slow motion as I eased her down under the water. I could see her close her eyes and take her last breath of air before the water washed over her. She went down slowly and I felt her body go limp under the water. I could feel all the trouble of life leaving in that water. I could feel that the water was literally washing the hardness of life right off her. I could feel the forgiveness given to her by Christ washing her clean. I could feel the Lord doing a miracle under that water. As I brought her back up, I saw dripping off her little droplets of water, taking the last bit of the world with them. She was literally being cleansed as forgiveness washed over her. I stood her up on her feet and she opened her eyes. She locked her eyes with mine and grabbed me and started to sob. She felt the Lord around us there also. She would forever be different and so would I. I could see the joy on her face and felt that same true joy in my soul.

I experienced something in that tank I had never realized before I saw the memory of it: I was helping someone take a step closer to

Christ and that gave me the greatest joy of my life. The Lord used me to do His work. I saw clearly what had taken place. I saw why He rushed through all my other memories of life and chose to stop at this one: what He wanted me to desire was working for Him. It was taking up my cross and really, deeply following Him. It was living so that others desired to follow Him as well. It was helping and guiding others to take their next steps with God. It was asking and praying every day to be used by Him to further His kingdom. It was walking so close with Him that if He turned, I would follow suit quickly. It was not following the world, because I would never be content; rather it was following Jesus and being content all my days. Where did He want me to go in life? What did He want me to do with my time? What did He want me to do with the money He gave me? How did He define prosperity for me? How could I be certain that I filled the rest of my life with kingdom moments like these?

The Changed Ones

The only way to answer those questions would be to ask Him, to seek Him, and to spend time with Him. He is the only One with the answers to what He wants from me, so I would have to ask Him. I would need to be in His word. I would ask Him to make my heart a new heart that desired only Him. I would spend my time with the TV off and His word in front of me. I would start giving my money back to Him and furthering His kingdom. I would ask Him how He defined success and start walking that direction. And if I did not know the way, or what He was saying, I would just grab His hand and silently walk with Him. I would seek His approval only and the approval of others would be insignificant. I would begin to let Him mold me into who He wanted me to be, where He wanted me to go, and what He wanted me to say. Jesus lives in my heart, so these hands are holy hands. That makes this mouth a holy mouth. That makes this body His temple. I desired to start to act and speak and walk like my Savior had taken up residence in me. I desired for myself to look like a changed one.

The Joy Seekers

I had met a few of these "changed ones" in the past. These people only attained fulfillment by working for the Lord. They lived joyfully because they worked for Him all of their days. Now, they had "normal" careers and lived "normal" lives to pay their bills and feed their families, but they frankly just didn't care about the trivial pursuit of "happiness." They searched out what gave them kingdom joy and they settled to do just that. These "joy seekers" floated around like they didn't want anything that everyone else wanted. They didn't see the importance of "stuff." There was something different about them. They met me in the halls at church and grabbed my arm and asked if I was okay when I had said nothing. They would lead me to the altar to help my walk with Jesus. They would be kind to me even when I was not kind to them. They listened to the Lord constantly to meet the needs of others. They talked about everything other than themselves. Actually, I couldn't get them to stop talking about Jesus. They knew His promises and could tell me why they loved Him. They had felt the chains of idle pursuit around their legs. They knew what freedom from the world tasted like. They knew how it looked. They lived free. Their life to me looked like they knew that their freedom costed someone their life.

Be the Change

I don't know if your life is all in following Jesus currently or not, but I think all of us would agree we always have room for improvement. I tried to sort it all out myself, but I needed His help. I first had to sit down in prayer with the Lord like I mentioned earlier. I asked for forgiveness for not following Him with my whole heart. I asked Him to reveal to me what to change about my life. I desperately wanted to show others the love that He first showed to me. I asked Him to convict my heart of things I shouldn't be pursuing. As I walked after this, He did convict me. On different days and at different times, I would feel the question, "Does this further my kingdom, Kristin?" And then I would work to change that.

Remember, the Lord holds the plans and we do not. Take His hand and walk away from the world. Take His hand and let Him guide you. It will most likely be somewhere that you have never gone before. He might bring you face to face with the things that hurt His heart. You might be overwhelmed by all that you've missed while standing idly by. This life is so much more than what the world tells you that it is. That heart in you was created to help other hearts be closer to Jesus. He has put different hearts in all of us. Some have a heart for the widowed, the elderly or addicts. Some have a heart for children or some have a heart for missions. My heart is for people hurting. My heart desires to help the people that are suffering. My heart wants to help people take steps out of chains and closer to Christ. I know what He wants me to do with my heart. He has turned me from wanting to be a part of the world, to wanting to be His heart *to* the world. What heart has He put in you? What gifts do you have to be able to work at the things that tug at His heart? You *do* have something to offer the kingdom of God. I am sure there is change in your church that you want to see. I am sure that there is change in your life, your home, and your community that you would like to see. Who is going to do it but you? What if the Lord has been waiting for you to change those things? You are brave enough to ask Him to make you the change He wants to see.

Walking Away Once and for All

It will be one of the hardest things that you will do when you decide to walk away from the world. No one will understand the pull to be out of the world unless they themselves have also exited. They could look at you with crazy eyes when you tell them that there is so much more to life than this. You will find the rest that only the Lord can offer when you find contentment in Him alone. You will begin to have a heart that is molded to help the weary. I know with all my being that He holds the plans for my tomorrow and that gives me rest. I have peace with the fact that this life will bring me tears, but I trust that He will hold me through it. In the moment when you decide that you do not want to be on the fence about this walking with Jesus thing, you will tighten your grip on His hand. When I decided that I wanted to follow Him with all my being, the things in the world no longer held any value to me. I allowed Him to make my mind new. I prayed to desire what He desired, I wanted to do His will, and I strived for my life to be acceptable to Him. "Do not conform to the pattern of this world, but be transformed by the renewing of your mind. Then you will be able to test and approve what God's will is- his good, pleasing and perfect will" (Romans 12:2).

You and I have to go into the world if we want to help people and bring them closer to Jesus. He says, "I have given them your word and the world has hated them, for they are not of the world any more than I am of the world. My prayer is not that you take them out of the world but that you protect them from the evil one. They are not of the world, even as I am not of it" (John 17:14–16). I know that I should feel out of place in this world just as Jesus did. This world was not His home and I cannot make it my home either. In times when I feel like I cannot make a difference, I am reminded that I am a child of God and He has chosen me to make a difference in His kingdom. He has overcome the world and I live in Him. I can do all He asks of me because my strength comes from Him. These words resonate in my soul when I so badly want to just give up: "You, dear children, are from God and have overcome them, because the one who is in you is greater than the one who is in the world" (1 John 4:4). What would the world be like if we lived like the One who lives in us is the One who has overcome the world? How would the world change if we all showed the light that was in us? The world would be a better place if His love radiated from us to the world, to the streets, to the sick and the weary, and to the oppressed and the suffering. Does it help those around you if you have a flashlight and only use it to light your own path? Does it help those around you if you have the light of God in your soul and only use it for your own good? If someone else's path is dark, would you be brave enough to lend them your lamp and share His word to light their way? You are either in the world, living as such, or you are not in the world, living as a light to it. You are brave enough to be a light to the world. That bravery comes from Him, and He is in you. Go, take His hand, follow Him wherever He would lead you, and be His light to the world.

Chapter 6

I Am Brave Enough to Let Him Choose My People

I WILL BE REFERRING TO people here that are true friends; people that we speak to frequently and deeply, people that we would call at midnight and they would rush over to help; people that would tell us when we were wrong; people that would fight for God's way in our lives; and people that we would consider our truest and closest friends, our "best friends," if you will; people that would be so close to us and our thoughts that they were able to hold us accountable at all times. This is about asking the Lord to help us to be surrounded by people in our most inner circles who want what the Lord wants for us. This is not about people that are just acquaintances. This is not about people that we just see occasionally and chat. This is about letting Him choose our *most* intimate and influential friends.

He Cares About Who Your Friends Are

I think it's pretty evident that God cared about who Jesus' friends were. If God did not want Jesus surrounded with those who loved Him, cared for Him, and helped Him, why would He have called up the disciples to stand next to Him? If God did not care about who Jesus surrounded Himself with, why summon up disciples? I know, you might think God called up His disciples to carry on His message after He died. If that was the sole purpose, God could have just made these men followers of Jesus and not true, close friends that He walked beside every day. He chose them to be His closest friends: the ones He leaned on, walked with, ate with, and prayed with. If He chose friends like this for Jesus, why would He not do this for us? I cannot help but believe that He cares for you and me in this same regard. After all, since He gave His Son to die for us, why would He not care about every single aspect of our lives? He didn't create us to see us flailing in the arena of friendship. He did not make us to be alone. He does not want us to be surrounded by people that tear us down and lead us to the ways of the world. He *hates* discord and did not create us to be surrounded with it. Our friends should bring us to God. We should bring them to God. They should not be afraid to call out sin and help us to forgive and move on with God. "Brothers and sisters, if someone is caught in a sin, you who live by the Spirit should restore that person gently. But watch yourselves, or you also may be tempted" (Galatians 6:1). They should always be encouraging us to remain faithful to God in all we say and do. "But encourage one another daily, as long as it is still called "Today," so that none of you may be hardened by sin's deceitfulness" (Hebrews 3:13). Being wise about our friends is a lesson learned at a very early age. I had a situation not too long ago that brought this to the forefront of my mind and taught me a great lesson about friendship, and in true Godly fashion, it came from someone I didn't think could teach me a lesson.

My daughter started coming home from school almost every single day with problems involving a friend. At first, I listened intently and gave her advice. I was caring and compassionate because I knew school could be rough. But then, she was coming home telling me the same story every single day. I talked to my daughter about what being a friend was and asked her if she needed to change some things about her way of being a friend. She admitted she did need to change some things like holding her tongue and being judgmental. I also told her that she needed to tell her friend what was wrong with their behavior and give her the chance to make a change. She told her. It helped for a day and then it was the same thing over and over again.

I know they are eight years old, and this wasn't the end of the world, but I also know that this potentially toxic friendship thing sometimes starts at a very early age. After many weeks of hearing about the same disrespectful behavior, I finally got fed up and told my daughter that her friend was always going to act like this and she needed to realize that. If she continued on with the friendship, she would do so knowing that this girl would probably hurt her again. She had to accept that. She said "okay" and I could tell she was disappointed at the realization that her friend might not be a good friend for her. We talked about all of it, together. I told her that most of the time we look around at people and deem them our "friends" almost instantly. We do not ask the Lord what He thinks of them. We do not ask Him what type of friend we need. Then, when they are not what we need, we try to bend over backward to make excuses for them not being a good friend. We tell ourselves they'll do better next time. We tell ourselves their selfish behavior will change with time. We might even change a lot about ourselves to please them. We could even bend our beliefs and morals to make them stay around. But sometimes no matter how much bending we do, we cannot fit their friendship into ours. It just will not work. I told her that this girl might not be a friend that the Lord would want for her. I told her that I knew that the Lord had His eyes on her and that she was loved. He had a friend in mind for her, but she would have to start praying to ask who it was. She would also need to seek how to be a good friend. She would need to read His word to find out what being a friend really was. In the end, I told her that maybe this girl would be a great friend to someone else, but for her, probably not. Was this sound parenting advice? I don't know, but I was doing that best that I could! I know that she was taught a great lesson and she was only a child. Maybe she would consult the Lord about her friends from then on. Hopefully, she would learn how to be a great friend to others herself just as the disciples learned this from Jesus and taught others. Maybe she would start to ask Him about everyone in her life. Praying about friends cannot start at too young an age. Asking God to give us good, Godly friends is a request we should bring before Him frequently and, at any age, in any season of life.

My Own Turning Point

If you are like me in any way, maybe you came to a point like I will tell you about here, or maybe you will sometime in your life. I woke up one day to discord and constant turmoil with my friends. I was unhappy with them and they were probably also unhappy with me. I was only surrounded with people that I had chosen for myself. Honestly, it's hard to imagine life a different way other than choosing our own friends, right? We think that we should get to decide who we surround ourselves with. We think we are smart enough to know who to choose. But the truth is we are not. I am not. We do not know what we need. We might think we do, but we don't. We are not God. We cannot see what kind of a friend we really need now or in the future. We cannot look ahead in time to know when people will cave under the pressure of friendship circumstances or stand with us when the going gets tough. We too often pick our own friends and then whine to God when they are not able to stand with us, let alone *for* us when He didn't even pick them for us in the first place. It is arrogant of us to say to God that we are able to pick our own friends. Frankly, I never knew what being a Godly friend meant, so how in the world could I pick one for myself? When was the last time I asked Him about my friends? When was the last time I asked Him to show me who to choose for a friend?

I asked these questions of myself because I knew something had to change about the people I surrounded myself with. I knew something had to change about me. Why was I surrounding myself will all this negativity? Why was that okay with me? Why was it okay that I asked the Lord about everything *but* my friends? I began to pray. I prayed that He would remove people from my life that He didn't want there. I prayed that He would allow me to desire the friends that He wanted for me. I prayed that He would make me strong enough to let people go. I prayed I would be brave enough to let Him choose my friends for me. But I realized that there were *a lot* of things about myself that I needed to change to be a good friend to others. I had to change some things so that He could send me who I needed because I was also going to be what they needed. I needed to see that I was not the most important thing in the world. My problems were monumental to me and that's okay, but there were others that needed help through their problems as well. The Lord told me that the friends He would send had been praying for a friend like me. I needed to know Jesus as my best friend in order to know what being a best friend really was.

Admittedly, I had to lose everyone to see what being a friend really was. And lose everyone I did. Over the course of a year or so the Lord allowed me to come to a place where everyone had grown away from me and I from them. For the first time in my life, I was all alone, no one to count on, no one to call, and no one to rescue me, except for the Lord. When I say that I was all alone, I really mean that. My husband was all I had. That was it. I did the only thing that I could do during this time and I called out to God. He was all I had in my corner. I had no one to rely on. I had no one to help me stand. I desperately needed a hand to hold and no one was there any longer. He had allowed everyone to walk away so that He could be all I needed. That season of loneliness was very much needed by me. Of course, I didn't know that then, but I would soon learn. I needed Him to teach me how to be a friend. I needed Him to give me good Godly friends that would lead me back to Him when I wandered off. I needed to learn that only He knows what's best for me. I needed to see that even though I think I know what people to call my best friends, I don't know at all. I needed friends who understood that He hates discord and they live accordingly. I needed prayer warriors for me and I for them. I needed Him to be a friend to me so that I could model what I saw.

I learned that He did not want me to be lonely. I was not meant to do this life alone, but that didn't mean I could pick whomever I wanted to surround me. When I finally had no one to lean on, I leaned on Him. He turned into my everything because He had to be. He had never been my everything before because I had so many "friends" to call on. I spoke to Him about my fears and my worries because I had no one to call. I spoke to Him about my insecurities and failures because no one else was there to talk to. I asked Him what to do about situations that arose in my life because, as I learned,

He knows better than anyone what is going on. I didn't call my closest friend because I didn't have one. I didn't ask anyone their opinion because I had no one to ask. I prayed about everything. I went to the Lord about everything. I didn't take a step without Him telling me to step. I learned how to live with God as my everything.

Guarding My Heart

Through this season of learning and growing with no one beside me but God, He revealed to me something that I had never seen before this: He had specific people that He wanted to help me, guide me, and keep me accountable. Before this great lesson, I saw that I was surrounded by so many people that I didn't need to reach out to the Lord when I had a problem. I had someone to call. I didn't go to the Lord in prayer because I had so many to pray for me. I didn't read His word because I had so many others to tell me what it said. I didn't stand on my own two feet because I was always being held up by others. I saw I had to fall. I had to fall down on my own, so that I would learn to stand with the Lord alone. I had to guard my heart and that, I learned, meant standing at the gate of my heart with the Lord, learning who should be granted access to it. There has to be a guard at your heart. Are you allowing the Lord to guard your heart and protect it? Are you allowing Him to be selective about who has access to your heart? Your heart needs a guard; are you equipped to know how to guard it? Are you brave enough to let Him stand at the door? It might be time to put another guard on duty.

What Is a Good, Godly Friend?

The only way to be Godly friend is to know what that looks like. The best example of friendship that we have is Jesus. He loves us unconditionally. It doesn't matter what we did or will do; He died on the cross for us no matter what. "But God demonstrates his own love for us in this: While we were still sinners, Christ died for us"

(Romans 5:8). He will never leave us or forsake us. "Be strong and courageous. Do not be afraid or terrified because of them, for the Lord your God goes with you; he will never leave you nor forsake you" (Deuteronomy 31:6). He will forgive us of any wrongdoing. 1 John 1:9 says, "If we confess our sins, he is faithful and just and will forgive us our sins and purify us from all unrighteousness." He will guide our ways. "I will instruct you and teach you in the way you should go; I will counsel you with my loving eye on you" (Psalm 32:8). Do we maintain friendships that teach and counsel us with a loving eye? Are our friends able to hold us accountable for our words and actions? What if we had friends that were all of these things that Jesus is to us? What if we ourselves desired to be all of things to our friends?

I promise that if you ask Him, He will put people in your life that are going to further your walk with Him. "Walk with the wise and become wise; associate with fools and get in trouble" (Proverbs 13:20). A good friend will tell you if your walk is going off His path. They will help to hold you accountable because, even if we are the most well-meaning people, we are often blinded by the enemy. I love this verse in Proverbs 27:6; it says, "Wounds from a friend can be trusted, but an enemy multiplies kisses." Wounds from a friend? Sounds like something I need in my life! Said no one ever. The simple truth is that a solid friendship is built on the understanding that a friend can, and hopefully would, tell you when you stepped out of line. "Whoever rebukes a person will in the end gain favor rather than one who has a flattering tongue" (Proverbs 28:23). Do you have friends like this? We are blinded every day by our own actions and thoughts. We cannot possibly see what others can see. The Lord allows people to see things and tell us what they see so that when He personally convicts us of something, we know how to listen to change. Have you ever lost a good friend because you reacted in anger to their honesty? Can you listen to your people around you? When is the last time that you were able to take some constructive criticism from a true friend? If you cannot trust your friends to be honest, how can you take honesty from the Lord? If you do not trust your true friends to be spiritually honest with you, what are they there for?

A Godly friend is going to lead you into spiritual wellness. They are going to say and do things that point you to Christ. They are going to make sure that you remain walking on the path with Jesus. They will try to give you honesty and truth to help to lead you to a deeper connection with Christ. I want you to be brave and ask the Lord what He thinks of your friends. I want you to be brave enough to take all of your friendships to the Lord and seek His counsel. Are your friendships leading you to be wise or are they leading you into trouble? Do you feel the love of God from the love of your friends? Can you believe that He loves you so much that He cares who your friends are? I want you to understand that He loves you so much that He wants to make sure you are surrounded by wise, caring, compassionate people. He loves you so much He wants to show you the kind of people He wants in your life to help you when you fall and to lift you up when times get hard. He wants to be able to give you wisdom about your circumstance through your friends. He wants to teach you how to be loyal through the loyalty of a friend. He wants to school you on how to accept constructive criticism so you will in turn accept it from Him with a glad heart. Above all, He wants to show you that you are so greatly loved through the undying love of a friend chosen by Him.

A New Way to Live

I will tell you now that every time I want to reach out and invite someone into my circle, I ask Jesus first. I pray over my choices. This means *everyone*. This is people at church that I spend a lot of time around. This is people from my past and new people for my future. I go over each and every single person in my life and ask the Lord about them, *every single person*. There are some people that I desperately want to allow back in, but the Lord says no. Some things I guess I will never understand.

I am learning to let Him guard my heart in a literal way like never before. I will walk like this for the rest of my life. I know what it looks like to be surrounded by people that the Lord did not choose and I never want to be there again. I am living a new life with new people now. I am learning how to be a Godly friend to those whom God chooses for me. I am consulting Him every day about my choices. He has planned goodness for me and now I am finally walking in that plan. I live life now with friends surrounding me that are chosen by God. Every time I feel myself wanting to go to a deeper level of friendship with someone, I go home and ask the Lord. I pray fervently that He would tell me if they are a right fit for friendship for me. Am I going to be a good fit for them as well? Will I be what they need? I will be honest, His answer to friendships is not always the answer I want, but I know that He knows who is best for me. I trust Him now.

I have never experienced friendship on this level before He chose my friends. I think bigger, love deeper, and forgive faster than I ever have before. I say I am sorry right when the Lord convicts me. (I used to be a grudge holder and I never apologized. With friends around me that tell me I have to say sorry and also do it themselves, I am learning quickly.) My friends now show me, not just preach to me, about how to act like Jesus. Do they fail? Yes, of course. Do I fail? Yes! Do we bicker and lose sight of Jesus in moments? Yes! We are human. But we always feel conviction from the Holy Spirit and we *act* on that conviction now. I need to see failure because if I see failure, I can see how they get up and I can learn from them. I myself have to fall to be able to allow the Lord to teach me how to stand. My friends and I do not hold anything from one another. These Godly women, we love each other with a very honest love. We do not sugar-coat our lives for each other. We are prayer warriors at all times for each other. We didn't find each other on our own accord. The Lord brought us all together in friendship. It's amazing what He did when I let Him be my guide in choosing friends. I realized soon after He established my new friends that these women are great pillars of the foundation of who He is. With these new friends around, even when times are hard and I cannot not feel Him or see Him, they remind me that He is near. They are His words to me and His love for me. They act out His love and show me He will never leave me.

A Tough Lesson While Walking in His Plan

As I walked with Jesus, He allowed me to be best friends with a woman whom I grew to love. I wanted her so badly to feel loved for the first time in her life. I wanted so desperately for her to know that someone cared about her. I tried very hard to convince her of this; always showing her how much I loved her, thinking she would feel Christ's love radiate through me. I didn't like to be pushy to people, especially when trying to explain the love of God. Besides, I think if I were honest, I would admit that His love is definitely something that you have to feel and not something that you can explain. I took more of an applied approach, thinking hopefully she would see something different in me. (I see now I should have spoken to her directly about the Lord, but I was scared back then.) I was the best friend to this woman that I could be. I was always there for her. I prayed for her and loved her with an honest love. In turn, she was always there for me. Right in the middle of this, the Lord told me my work was done. "I'm sorry, Lord. I don't think that I heard you correctly. You're asking me to step away from this woman? I don't understand how you just want me to leave. Then I will be no different than everyone else in her life! I will be another one that walked away. I will be nothing. Everything that I have done will be pointless, a complete waste of my time!" I didn't want to listen and step away, so I tried harder. I did know how to listen to the Lord at this point, but listening and then doing what He says are two completely different things. I knew He wanted me to move on, but Satan was telling me if I moved on, I would be a failure to her. Why in the world would someone walk away from a friend for no reason?

I forgot that He had walked the path before me and He knew what it looked like. I failed to put into use what I already knew: sometimes in life, we get to be the planter, the one who plants the seeds of love and faith. We might not be around to watch it grow, but we helped plant it. Other times, we get to be the one who waters the plant. We didn't tell someone about Christ (plant the seed), but we get to help them on their walk and bring them closer to Him. Other times, we get to see them bloom. We get to see them be all they can be! We get to see them realize the love that the Lord has for them.

By accepting these truths in my life about my purpose in the lives of others, I realized that His will for friendships in my life may not always be lifelong. My plan for this friend was not to be the one who saw her bloom or even the one who watered her seed of faith. I was merely the planter and my work was done. It was very difficult to accept this, but I realized through conviction that if I stayed, she would never bloom. It ended rather harshly because I had not stepped away when the Lord had originally asked me to. If I had listened at the beginning, I would have been able to explain what was happening and I know she would've understood because she knew I loved her. I messed up the whole thing by not listening to Him telling me to step back. It was a learning moment for sure, a lesson about listening that I will never forget, a lesson that His timing was perfect and I had to trust that with my whole heart, even when I did not understand. I had to be brave enough to let her go. I had to be brave enough to trust that as much as He had a plan for me, He also had a plan for her. Being brave enough to step away meant that I had great faith in the One who I knew would guide her.

Applying These Lessons to Your Own Life

Who are you walking with? Do you live for God or do you live for man? "For am I now seeking the approval of man, or of God? Or am I trying to please man? If I were still trying to please man, I would not be a servant of Christ" (Galatians 1:10). We sometimes hang on to friendships for years trying to please someone other than God. Someone once said, "Tell me who your friends are and I will show you who you are." How true is this! The Lord loves you so much that He has great people ready and lined up for you. He will lead you to unwavering love. He will teach others how to be a friend to you and teach you how to be a friend to others. Today is the day to make the choice to live for the approval of God and let Him choose your closest friends.

Chapter 7

I Am Brave Enough to Be Guilty by Association

My Witness

Who will know I know you, Lord?
Who can see your face?
Are my hands your hands,
are my feet your feet,
or is my witness a big disgrace?
My sister knows, my mother knows,
but what of the man on the street?
Does he see my eyes always looking toward heaven?
Can he see something different in me?
I don't want to look like everyone else, Lord,
I want to walk and talk and act like you,
so my actions scream your name.
This world, Lord, has nothing for me,
Not a home, nor shoes, nor fame.
Make me look like you Lord,
So the man on the street knows your name.

WHO ARE YOU? HOW do you define yourself? If you had to make one top ten list of the things that define you, what would you put down? Go ahead, make the list, and rank them as one being the thing that defines you most and then down to ten. Make the list on a piece of paper so you can look at it before you go on. I'll wait here. Okay, what is your number one thing that defines you? When I first made my list, the number one thing that defined me was "mom." Although being defined as a mother was not bad at all, I was missing something. "Follower of Jesus" ranked number four. Yes, I am a mother. I am a business owner. I am a volunteer. I am a wife. I am a follower of Jesus. Those were part of *my* list. But, more importantly than all those things, I am saved by the blood of Christ and I chose Him as my Savior. Therefore, I am a member of the body of Christ. 1 Corinthians 12:27 says, "Now you are the body of Christ, and each one of you is part of it." The Lord spoke to me and told me that being "a part of the body of Christ" should have been my main definition of myself. But, why? What I failed to see was that if everything else was taken away, I would have still been defined as a member of the body of Christ. If the number one definition of myself was "a member of the body of Christ," then the idea of knowing who I was and where my identity laid would be clear. As a member of the body of Christ, my job was to spread the gospel of Jesus Christ. Point blank. That should have been the back-breaking, shoes-to-the-pavement, go-get-em-reason-that-I-lived definition of who I was. But, it wasn't. Something was wrong.

If something happened to my children, my number one definition would have been lost. If I was not a volunteer any longer, my list would have been altered. What if my business went under? How would I define myself then? I would have been wondering how in the world I would function with my number one definition ripped out from underneath me. My life would have careened out of control. I would have been flailing in the catastrophe of no longer having a definition for myself. You know how I know this would've happened? Because it did. I had gotten to a point where all I thought about was my business. It was all I could see, feel, and do. I worked every single day toward the goals that I had set and toward dreams that I dreamed for myself. I sought the Lord less and less as I ran down the path blazed by myself. I left the Lord standing in my dust. I didn't need Him anymore because I was not working for Him; I was working for me. I did not need to talk about Him anymore because He was not on my mind. I did not need to tell people about Him because I was telling them about me. Why would I need to talk with Him every day when I did not need His wisdom in my life? I was relying on my own wisdom to take me to a place that He had no desire for me to be. My big business dream was not the dream that He had for me. His immediate plan for me was this book and He needed my heart completely devoted to Him to be able to write it. I would have to seek Him every day to be able to know what to write. I would have to know when He was speaking and what He was saying. I would need to know where to step next. I would need to be in His presence every single day. I would need to know who it was that I was working for. I would need to realize exactly who was to be praised for this life; and that person was not me. I needed a wake-up call in my life to see just who it was that I was really living for. I needed someone to jostle my mind lose from the self-centered reality that I knew as home for far too long because it was not just affecting me; it was affecting everyone I came into contact with.

The Dream

I needed to see that a calling to work in even the smallest of ways for the kingdom is working something big for Him. I needed to see that my heart should break when His does. I needed to see just how important it was to show everyone that I was a member of the body of Christ. Above all, I needed to become keenly aware of what my life was showing people and what desperately needed to be changed. I read and felt His commands from His word in my heart. Now I needed to see firsthand what my life looked like to others and to Him so that I could faithfully walk where my feet had never gone before.

My eyes were opened one hot summer night in June. I had a dream. I was walking down a very busy street. The street was familiar to me like the main street of the small town I grew up in. I started to realize that the only people in this town were people that had crossed my path in life. There were people I had grown up with, people that I had known from work, and people that I went to church with. Everyone that I had ever come across in my life was walking around. Yes, everyone. These "random people" made up the mass number of people in this town. There were very few that knew me personally but thousands that knew me just for a moment. As I began to peer at everyone's faces, it took me just seconds to decipher who they were. There was the cashier who took my money at McDonald's. There was the woman on the other end of line at the phone company. (I obviously had never seen her face, but I knew her now.) There was the woman at the grocery store who asked me if I was having a good day. (I was in fact not having a good day that day.) There was the receptionist at the doctor's office, all my clients, and the man who cut me off on the road. There was my waiter at the restaurant. There were my daughter's teachers. There was the girl who taught her tumbling class. There was my children's doctor. There were all my "friends" and "followers" from social media. Oddly enough, even if I had never seen their faces before, I knew each and every one of them and where I knew them from. In that same respect, everyone knew me. They also knew who I was walking with; I just felt that. They all knew that the man walking with me was Jesus. He was standing very close to me, holding my hand as I peered into everyone's eyes.

As I turned my attention from the Lord, I felt people staring at me, like when you can feel someone's eyes boring into the back of your head, yeah, that feeling. One woman came up to me, touched my arm, and whispered, "I didn't know you were friends with Him" (eye roll to Jesus). She looked at Him with disgust and she walked off. She wanted nothing to do with Him. I was so embarrassed that she didn't know I was friends with Him and my face said that. I was red from my toes up. I stopped dead in my tracks. I didn't say a word; I just turned to look at Jesus. He said nothing, only looked to me. Just then, He turned my attention to the road behind us. We had been walking together for a very long time. All my life was behind us. I had come across so many people. I looked at all those people that I had come into contact with on my walk. I was in complete awe at the number of people, people that I didn't even remember coming into contact with, people that I didn't even know were listening to me talk, and people that I didn't even know were watching me walking with Him. Was it apparent to this mass of people that I loved Jesus? As we walked on, I looked at the faces around me. Some were smiling like they knew why I was with Jesus, and some were perplexed. Come on people, I go to church every week! I post "Christian" things on social media, I pray before I eat, I give God the glory for my blessings, and I volunteer at church!

I could feel us walking to the courthouse. Don't ask me how I knew this; I just knew. My palms began to sweat and adrenaline started pumping through my veins. I didn't know why we were going there, but just the thought made me so uneasy. We walked in together. Someone separated us, and the Lord took His seat at the front and I also took mine. It was like my body knew what was going on and where to sit, but my mind did not. In the time it took for me to drop His hand and go to my seat, I realized why we were there. It only took me a second as I glanced around to know: I was on trial for being a follower of Jesus. The room went dim and my ears started to ring. I was frozen in panic.

They had already arranged all the witnesses before we came in. They wasted no time in getting started. They called person after person after person to the witness stand. They asked them: Does she talk like she knows Jesus? Does she act like she knows Jesus? Does she talk about Him like they're friends? How much time do you think she spends with Him? Has she ever told you about Him? Does she love you like He loves her? I started sobbing as their answers were no, no, no, maybe once a week at church, no. I wanted to be guilty. I wanted to be guilty if only by association. My loved ones took the stand. I'm saved, I thought! They will surely find me guilty after my family speaks! My hope quickly diminished as they each took the stand. In all of their answers, I realized I show the love of Jesus more to strangers than I do toward my own family. Their answers were like taking a knife to my core. I wanted to run. I told Jesus over and over and over how much I loved Him, but I failed to show the world the love He first showed to me. My actions did not show many people that I walked with Jesus. My speech did not tell many people that I talked with Jesus. Of the thousands upon thousands of people I came across in my life, there were only a few that said with certainty that I walked with Jesus. These people were not being malicious to me. They were not out to take me down. They were just being honest in this courtroom. They honestly did not know that I walked with Jesus. They never felt that love from me. They never heard His name come out of my mouth.

The judge looked at me when everyone had spoken. The verdict was in. He told me I was found "not guilty" and I could leave. I jumped up and yelled that I *was* His friend! I spoke to Him every day! I wanted to be just like Him! The judge spoke, "Ma'am, it was evident by what we had heard today that you told no one about this Jesus but a select few, thus telling me and this court that you had not been proud to be His friend. Everyone who has testified could name all your other friends but Him. You did not let anyone know that you followed this man. Your acquaintances and friends and family have spoken otherwise. For that reason, you can go." I stood with my mouth gaping open and my hands held high in confusion. I turned and looked behind myself as the tears streamed down my face. I was completely devastated. I could not plead my case. I could not make the judge see things the way I saw them. I could not reverse time. The Lord could not return with me, for there were more people to stand trial that day. Would any of them be guilty? The judge informed me on my way out to stick close to the courtroom because I would be called back as a witness for others I had known. I began to think of people I would be called for. What would I say? I have to be honest. I have to tell them what I have seen and what I have heard from them. I would have to say if I thought they knew Jesus.

The truth is this is life. This is reality. We are given many chances every single day to just show people Jesus in one way or another. We are given so many opportunities to show people the love that Jesus has shown to us. We are given so many chances to show the kindness that Jesus has shown us. We are given the opportunity to show the forgiveness that He has given to us. The fact is we do not deserve what He gives us and yet He gives it anyway. Likewise, there are so many people that don't deserve our kindness, that don't deserve our forgiveness, that don't deserve to be rescued, that don't deserve our prayers, and that don't deserve one ounce of our time. Since we are the body of Christ, we have a great responsibility to show *everyone* Jesus. We have a great responsibility to heed His commands without question. Will we meet Him every day in prayer and then keep Him to ourselves? Will we never share with people all the reasons why we love Him so? What do we do with this authority given to us? Do we squander it because Satan tells us people will think we're crazy if we look, talk, and act like Jesus?

I felt complete shame that day that I got off free. I did not walk away full of dignity. I walked away disgraced. On the way out, I turned to look at Jesus through my red, puffy, crying eyes. I just glanced over my shoulder. As I turned around, I saw that He was already looking at me. His eyes had been on me, watching me the whole time as I walked away. His eyes were also full of tears. He mouthed that He loved me. I was frozen with my hand on the door handle. He loved me? How could He love me after all of that? How could He even want to look at me knowing what I hadn't done? How could I ever stand with Him again? I could feel Satan push the door open for me and he turned as I did, walking out with me in stride. "You are terrible," he said to me. "What a follower you are. No one even knew you knew Him. You might as well get out of this Christian thing and go back to living for you. The world has so much to give you. You don't know what you're missing. You should feel awful. You are an awful person. He might say that He loves you, but He is so ashamed of you."

As I walked out, I thought of Jesus and I asked Him to tell me His truth. I was being lied to and I needed to hear who I really was. I felt worthless in this moment. I saw His face when He looked at me in that courtroom. To Him I looked righteous. He knew what was coming when He held my hand as we walked into this courtroom, and He held it anyway. His blood that was shed on the cross had transformed me into something beautiful in His eyes, something that He, in all His majesty, could stand to look at. I was beautiful in His sight. I was a human who sinned and He already covered that. There was nothing that I had done that He wouldn't forgive. I was loved and forgiven. I just didn't deserve a speck of it. It was mine and I was going to hold onto it. I was given a second chance. My eyes were opened and I was not going to ruin this second chance. I was going to show people my Jesus.

Lessons Learned

Looking back, I see now that I was so worried about the things that I could say to point people to Jesus that I forgot that most days my actions toward others spoke mountains more than my mouth. I wondered throughout conversations when I would be able to get something in about Him. What can I say to make people see Jesus? I got so caught up in thinking about what I could say that I forgot about what I could do. Satan left me in a mental dance off with him about what I should be saying all the time! The more I was asking Jesus to speak, the more I was missing the Holy Spirit speaking to me! I didn't have to ask Him to speak; if I was listening, I would hear it whenever He spoke. The truth is I was so busy thinking about what I would say about Jesus that I missed what He was saying to me. I missed that He might tell me to act in a way that would point people to Him. I missed that being a member of the body of Christ was not always about talking about Jesus but being a witness for Him in all ways and doing what He commands without hesitation. I realized that I had been so worried and wrapped up in where I was going in life that I forgot that my purpose was to show people Jesus. The Lord was making my path cross with so many others on my journey, but I was too busy with my dreams to even see that they were there.

How are we showing Jesus to the world without our plans getting in the way? How do we not miss a moment that He set up for us to work for His Kingdom? People will see it in many ways. They see it in the way we talk about others. They see it in the way we go out of our way to help others. They see it in the way we actually walk and not in the way we *say* we walk. Showing people Jesus is giving them what they don't deserve, showing people Jesus is loving on them when there's not a part of them that deserves it, showing people Jesus is having a peace beyond all understanding in the midst of terrible circumstances, and showing people Jesus is being joyful in the midst of the storm. At the same time, it is showing them that knowing Jesus does not make us perfect and knowing Jesus does not make our lives easy. Actually, knowing *and* following Jesus make our lives sometimes more difficult. It makes our circle very, very small. It makes us feel like an alien in the world. It might make people run from us. This should be the truth about following Jesus: If we truly follow in the ways of Jesus Christ, the love we have for Him should take authority over *all* others (Luke 14:26). We will be hated by the world (John 15:18–19). We will give up anything and everything we possess to follow Jesus (Luke 14:33). We will give up the things that we want, to desire the things the Lord wants (Luke 9:23). We should be able to die to ourselves and be fully obedient to Christ so that all we say and do points others to Him.

You Have a Calling

As members of the body of Christ, the Lord gives us all gifts to use. The enemy lives to try to make us believe that we are not given a gift. If we believe that we do not possess a gift from the Lord to further His kingdom, then why would we try to find it? We wouldn't, right? The gift that He has for all us will help us narrow down what our part is in the body of Christ. These gifts given to us by God all work together in the body. Is one gift more important than another? Not at all. There are many parts in the body, but regardless we are one body. "If one part suffers, every part suffers with it; if one part is honored, every part rejoices with it" (1 Corinthians 12:26).

Sometimes we can fall into the trap of looking at people who are using their gift in a big way and think that our gift isn't as import-ant. I have looked up to the stage of my pastor and thought that my work will never be as big as his. I have held little babies in the church nursery and thought my work is not doing anything huge for God. I have wondered if telling people of the Lord is really doing any good. Have you also heard these lies? I'm going to tell you the actual truth

and I want you to write it down and carry it with you: *you were created with a purpose and a gift to be used by God, no matter how small
you think you are.* "For we are God's handiwork, created in Christ
Jesus to do good works, which God prepared in advance for us to do"
(Ephesians 2:10). You may never have heard that before. You may
have heard it and thought that it doesn't apply to your life. You may
have heard it and tried to accept it and failed. It sounds so simple, but
yet it is sometimes so difficult for us to believe that we have gifts and
God has a plan to use those. If Satan is able to distort any of God's
truths in our lives, he agitates the solid foundation that the Lord has
laid. The lies that he tells us seem so small and insignificant in the
moment, but over time this steady agitation of our foundations leads
to our spiritual demise and the breakdown of our God-laid footing.
Some of you have been there. Some of you are there now. I was
exactly right there also. I didn't know that my enemy had convinced
me that I was meaningless and that I had nothing to show for God.
He was tearing down my foundation. Every brick in our foundation
laid by God is a brick of His truth. Every time the enemy convinces
us that one of his lies is in fact truth, he takes a brick from our foundation in God. We can all see where this would end.

My enemy convinced my heart that I in some way was weak
and insignificant to the Lord. But a truth brick that was laid in
my foundation told me that, "Even so the body is not made up of
one part but of many" (1 Corinthians 12:14). The truth is that *we
all* play a part. There is not one person that is weak and insignificant. All of the people in the body work together to further His
kingdom. No one is more important than another, for if it wasn't
for all the parts, we would fail. Just because we are not called to
be pastors in front of huge throngs of people does not mean that
we are not just as important as them in the body. "Now if the
foot should say, 'Because I am not a hand, I do not belong to the
body,' it would not for that reason stop being part of the body"
(1 Corinthians 12:15). Since we should define ourselves by being
part of the body of Christ first, we have to be aware that He has a
plan for us bigger than any plan we could imagine for ourselves,
bigger than being a mother, bigger than the job promotion, big-

ger than being a business owner, bigger than being a wife, and bigger than being successful. All of our gifts bring glory to the Father and lead ourselves and others to Him. Each and every single gift is to be used to tell and show others who God is.

"But you will receive power when the Holy Spirit comes on you; and you will be my witnesses in Jerusalem, and in all Judea and Samaria, and to the ends of the earth" (Acts 1:8). I think the Bible makes it clear that His mission is to show the love of the Father to all humanity. That is the witness that I want to be and that is where my gifts will come into use. Are you missing a grand opportunity to show the love of Christ to the world because you don't think you have the feet to take you there? Do you not have the hands that know how to work for the Lord?

You Can Be Guilty

Don't get me wrong, being a follower of Jesus takes practice and teaching from Him. You will never be perfect. I will never be perfect. Man, sometimes it feels as though I fail multiple times every day. But I know now that I was not made to stay put when I fail. I was not made to spiritually be at the same place today that I was three years ago. I was made to be so much more than a substitute waiting to go into the game. The desire to be guilty by association starts with you and your heart. The moment that you decide that you solely desire to show Jesus to the world is the moment He will start to change your life. He will make you desire what He desires. He will make your heart hurt for what hurts His heart. Just start by telling Him you desire Him and only Him. "Lord make me only desire for you today." Let Him change you. You will not be able to change your walk yourself. It could take a while for the Lord to bring to the surface all He wants to change in you, but I promise it's worth it. I know for me it took years for the Lord to purify some things from my life. I want your desire to walk with Jesus to be burning hot inside your soul. I want you to be able to hear the voice of the enemy. I want you to be able to distinguish when you have dropped the hand of Jesus.

I want you to feel different than everyone around you. I want you to feel like you are not home here on this earth. I pray everyone sees Jesus in you. I pray you decide to live guilty of *knowing* and *walking* with Jesus. Do you desire to be guilty? Prove it.

Section 2

Strong: Able to Withstand Great Force or Pressure

Chapter 8

I Am Strong Enough to Accept There Will Be Pain

NOTHING ABOUT GOD HAS changed or ever will change. "For I the Lord do not change…" (Malachi 3:6). I have heard people say that the God that existed two thousand years ago is not nearly the same God that exists today. They point at the world and call me crazy for thinking we serve the same God today. Maybe even as a Christian, you tend to think that. You can't see any miracles, right? No one is parting seas nowadays. No one is making burning bushes talk. No one is raised from the dead. We look at what God did and said back then and we don't see anything that even remotely resembles that today. Where is that hand of God today? Why doesn't He bring us out of the fire unharmed? Do you yourself believe that He is not the same? This mode of thought will infect your soul little by little. It's like a virus that slowly makes its way around every cell in your soul. It will make you believe that He cannot do all the things that He says He can do. It will make you start to check out of praying. It will make you start to dislodge your hand from His. *If you believe that the God of today isn't the same, why would you care to hold the hand of Him who doesn't hold the same mighty power?* You might say He has left humanity to their own devices. "Peace-out world," there He went. You can almost see Him closing the door to heaven as His foot crosses the threshold. "Look at all the terrible in the world and tell me God is still here!" you say! And I would say, "look at all the terrible in the world and tell me that evil doesn't exist to destroy all the good that God creates!" Satan doesn't want us to believe that God has any power today and I would venture to say that he has convinced much of humanity that this is truth! People aren't building arks and walking through fire or sleeping peacefully with lions, so we think that God has taken a backseat. "The world is too bad and He called it quits. He doesn't love us the same anymore. He is not big enough to take care of all of it." Satan has lied to us and filled our heads with so much nonsense that we believe we are better off on our own! If you think for a second that you are better off on your own, Satan has accomplished his main objective, making God look and feel so small that you think you do not need Him in your life.

Has he successfully done this in your life? Have you been deceived enough to believe the same God as two thousand years ago does not exist today? Have you walked away from Him because you cannot see miracles performed in your own life or lives of the ones you love? Miracles that you think *should* be performed on your behalf? Satan has been successful then. He has convinced you that you are better off on your own. You're out there flailing in water just an inch above your nose. You have put all of your trust in yourself, but you cannot save yourself. The water will continue to rise until at some point it will overtake you. The truth is that God did not promise a life without pain. Has the enemy told you pain means God left you? He did not promise that you wouldn't have heartache, grief, or suffering. Sin entered the world a long time ago and changed the course of humanity. Just because awful things are happening does not mean the Lord checked out. Who lied to you and told you a life with pain is a life apart from God? What good can come out of your suffering? What good can you do with it? Who can you be an advocate for? Who can you reach with your story? Who can you pull from the depths, the same depths that you also have been in? "I consider that our present sufferings are not worth comparing with the glory that will be revealed in us" (Romans 8:18).

I am not telling you that sometimes life just doesn't seem fair. I am not telling you to quit whining about your pain. I am not telling you that you should just toughen up. I have felt deep pain. So many people walk around with pain from suffering that no one even has a clue they went through. I wonder how our minds would change toward people if we wore our hurt on the outside. Then we would know right away others' suffering. Some people have shocking pain. Honestly, some of us wouldn't be able to sleep just hearing the pain that others have gone through.

How we react to our pain is the game changer. What we do with the pain is the fork in the road. Do we use it to help someone else? Do we hide it away and punish ourselves forever? Do we use it as the fuel in our spiritual gas tank to be mad at God? Do we allow it to purify our hearts and bring to the surface things that need sifted out? What do we learn from our hurt? How can we use it to help others or even ourselves?

From Pain Comes Strength

There was a time in my life that my pain was deep and I lived in it every single day. Did I bring this on myself? No. Could I control what was happening to me? No. Was the Lord punishing me for something? No. I was doing what He wanted me to do! I was listening to His voice! We were on this road together! What was happening to us? I had just had my first child. I felt it right away. The second the nurses laid my child on my chest, I felt like I wanted to run. I was overcome with the greatest anxiety that I have ever known. I remember thinking I was supposed to cry. Everyone around me was watching to see me cry with joy. So, I did. But those tears weren't what everyone thought they were; they were tears of anxiety and life-altering fear. I cried in the hospital. I cried at home. I worried constantly. Literally, not one second of the day could I maintain a clear thought. I was a prisoner in my own mind. I was chained to my thoughts, living defeated each and every day. "Where are you God? Why have you left me when I needed you most?" I was sick. My hormones were out of control! My body just couldn't bounce right back like all the other women that I knew. Why didn't the Lord just take this from me? Why did He even let it happen in the first place? Satan used what my body was going through as an open door to lie to me in the biggest way that I have ever experienced. I wasn't good enough. I wasn't strong enough. My faith wasn't where it should be. I didn't love Him enough. I was a failure. I would be a terrible mom. There were so many women who wanted to be moms and here I was saying thanks but no thanks! I was a terrible person. I believed each and *every one* of these lies. I didn't want to wake up the next day and feel that anymore. If that was going to keep up, I was checking out. I fell into deep despair. I laughed and smiled at everyone on the outside and hurt so deeply on the inside. Satan convinced me that my family would be better off without me. I believed that the Lord had checked out. I did not believe that He was who He said He was. He was not a big God since He didn't take away my pain. Why wasn't He stepping in and rescuing me? Why didn't He take it all away from me? Why couldn't I just be a joyful mother? My husband was nervous to leave me to go back to work. He was confused and didn't know how to deal with that. I was failing everyone. As a human, my body was going through something it had never gone through before. My spiritual side was not strong enough before this to counter the lies I was hearing. I was deceived and I hid it in my heart so deep that even if someone wanted to help, they would never have been able to. What I had on my hands was a train wreck.

I was walking down a small hall in my house and stopped to let the wall brace me. I felt the wave coming. I began to sob. I was going to decide what I was going to do. I didn't want to go on like this anymore. I literally could think of nothing besides the anxiety and turmoil I felt inside. I finally collapsed. I cried out to a Lord that I wasn't sure was there anymore. I cried out to a God that I hoped was hearing me. I cried out so deeply. I was locked inside a box of defeat. As far as I was concerned, there was no way out. I didn't go one second of the day without thinking about my fears. I didn't eat or sleep or take a shower without thinking about them. My stomach was in knots all the time. I wanted to just feel like this would end. I was on the ledge and I wanted to die. I wanted to just know that somehow, someway, this would get better and death was the only way out. I crawled to my couch and got on my knees *one last time*. Literally,

He was the only tiny bit of hope that I had. He was the only thing that could help me out of this. I couldn't hear anything from Him. I couldn't feel Him move. I listened as hard as I could for anything. I heard the enemy tell me that I should never have been a mother. My child did not deserve a mother like this. "Oh, my gosh, that's right," I said out loud. "I should never have been a mother. I don't know why the Lord thought I was strong enough for this." I was sobbing uncontrollably. My hands were shaking. My head was throbbing. I faintly heard His voice in the background of my ferocious mind.

"I love you."

My eyes darted around. My breathing slowed. My tears stopped flowing. "What did you say?" I whispered.

"I love you," He said again.

My eyes had begun to open wide at the sound of His truth. I seriously had forgotten how much the Lord really loved me. I was believing that all this pain meant that He didn't love me anymore. Truths were flooding my foggy mind: God had chosen me for this job. He had chosen me to be this child's mother. He knew something about me that I didn't know. He knew that I could be a wonderful mother. He knew the things that laid inside of me. He brought back the memories of when we found out I was pregnant. I was so happy. I saw my smile. We called everyone. I remembered the shock and smile on my husband's face. I recalled the joy of our parents. He had, in fact, chosen me for this role. Regardless of what my body was doing right now, there was a purpose to this life of mine. There was a purpose for my today and tomorrow and the next. I had to be this child's mother. I was chosen for this. His truth was flooding my soul and I felt myself want to rise up! I cannot explain the power that came to me in these moments. I cannot accurately tell you how I felt so low and so powerful at the same time. He did not remove the anxiety and depression from my mind. He merely allowed His love to take precedence over them. Like lightning that hit me from the head down, I was burning hot inside my soul with the true love of Jesus. I had always heard that His love changes things but now it literally was changing my decision to want to keep on.

I started to ask the Lord every single day for help. I cried out to Him all day long in the midst of it all. My prayers would always be for healing, but now I also prayed for strength to endure. I prayed that He would show me His love regardless of my circumstances. He gave me that strength every single day. I knew I wouldn't be able to do this alone like I had been doing. I finally reached out to Christian women that had been walking with Jesus in the midst of depression and anxiety for years. I wanted to know how they kept going on. I found that they lived each day putting one foot in front of the other. Some days were harder than the others. Some days they just cried out to Him and other days they were soaring! But they all believed with everything in their being that they were loved despite the pain. He promised to never leave us; He didn't promise a life without pain.

God used that awful time in my life to show me how close He was to me. I know that sounds completely crazy to you. I see how that doesn't sound right. I felt so alone and yet He was so close? Yes. I wanted to die and yet He was there? Yes. In this situation in my life, I would look back and see that although He allowed me to go through this, He was so close to me while in the middle of it. He was beside me whispering that He loved me when I didn't want to live. He was that very quiet voice in my heart that told me it wasn't worth it. He told me I was being lied to. I remember hearing all that now as I look back. By bringing me through this, He showed me He would be there even in the darkest valley. I had never known the true strength of God until those moments. I did not understand who it was that I followed up until then. Before this, I read His promises in a way that grazed the top shell of my heart. While going through this and after this, I read those promises and let them permeate my heart. Those promises finally took up residence in my heart. I finally felt them deep in my soul. I can look people square in the eyes now and tell them God is with them and believe it from the bottom of my soul. My pain was not a gauge of His love for me. I thought I knew so much about God before this. I thought I knew Him. I thought I loved Him. I realize now that the closer that I got to Him through my pain, the less I really needed to know about the time frame of my circumstances. And that's freeing.

Rising Above Circumstances

I have a good friend that has been in terrible, awful, literal pain most of her adult life. You would never guess this looking at her. She is beautiful and smiles a lot because she knows how to fake being happy on the outside while torn apart on the inside. Most of us do, don't we? She's had years of practice. She looks like a tough nut to crack. When I first met her, the Lord whispered to me that she was in pain. I knew what that meant because I had heard Him say it many times before; her heart was hurting, and she needed Him. Nearly most every day, she cannot take a step without terrible pain. When her children were young, she couldn't even walk on her feet, her own feet! She spent most of all of her life mad at the Lord, right where the enemy wanted her. He backed her into a corner and then built walls around her suffering and pain. She was all alone, all the time. She was controlled by her chains of anger and resentment from the pain. "If the Lord your God loves you, then why would He do this to you? If He hears your prayers, then why doesn't He relieve your pain? How can anyone want to serve a God like this? You're better off without Him," the enemy told her. How could a God that loves her so much allow her so much pain for so long? Why wasn't He answering her prayers of healing? I was honest with the only thing that I knew for sure in that moment she was with me. I didn't have the answers and she might not ever know those answers this side of heaven. That was my truth for her. I wasn't going to tell her it would all be okay, because really, what amount of pain is "okay"? That's kind of a vague statement anyway. Her pain might never be okay; her circumstance might not ever be okay. She might not ever know the why to make it "okay." Satan would have her run in circles her whole life chasing the why. One thing I did know was that in the midst of her pain, she could live in truth. She could live in victory over her pain. That needed to be her truth. I prayed for a long time about telling her His truth.

When I finally blurted out one day to her that Jesus loved her, she looked at me with tears in her eyes. She couldn't believe what I was saying. Her face said that she potentially wanted to smack me.

How dare I say that to her! How could I tell her that she was loved by someone who allowed her to live in such awful circumstance? She didn't know my story. She didn't know the prison from which I was freed. I was loved in the midst of pain and I knew she was too. She had listened to the enemy for so long she didn't believe me. I said it again, and again, and again. She left that night not at all believing what I said. I told her every day that she was loved. I told her in the morning, I told her at night, and I told her when I thought of it. I told her when she didn't want to hear it, but I waited until prompted by the Holy Spirit so I didn't chase her farther away. She soon started to think maybe, just maybe, He did love her despite her pain. It was just that small moment in time that she felt the Lord move. She felt the Lord's love when I told her time and time again that she was loved. Something "clicked." The sun shined just a tiny bit for the first time in so many years. The fire in her heart was being fanned. She was greatly loved no matter anything else. Who was she? Who was she created to be? What was she helping sitting here in this corner? Who is this enemy that has kept her chained here for so long not allowing her to live?

That was it. How long had she been here? How much had she missed in this prison? Who had she chased away while here? How many words from the Lord had she missed over the years? She got up and out of the corner. She put up her fists and decided to fight for this life. She only gets one shot at this. She decided to fight her way out of the enemy's chains. She was going to take back her life, pain or no pain. She realized Satan wanted her to remain in that corner alone, angry, and afraid all the days of her life. She was mad at him now for convincing her that she wanted to live in anger. His only goal was that she remained mad at God for her circumstance. She realized in that very moment how long he had succeeded and it made her sick. He managed to convince her that this was all life had for her. Her fire was beginning to get bigger. She felt the Lord tell her to move! He did not create her to be in chains! He did not create her to be angry or resentful. He did not create her to be disgraced or shameful. He created her to simply be loved and love in return, no matter the pain or her circumstance. She refused to live resentful and

98

angry any longer. She refused to listen to the enemy telling her she wasn't loved. She felt the Lord dying for her. She knew He suffered for her. She knew He was in agony and died a brutal death so she could live in victory over the enemy! She stepped over the line. She made the choice. She learned His love was not defined by how much pain He takes away. His love was not defined by how much pain He keeps away from her. His love for her is defined by Him dying on a cross so she could live a life of freedom from the chains of the enemy; chains of a life apart from God.

Although she is still learning to live like a victorious woman, she knows she can live with joy in the midst of pain. The Lord has not taken her pain away even to this day as I write this, and yet she is more joyful than she ever has been. You say you don't see miracles today? I do. She now prays for others' suffering and tries to show people her joy so they can live free. People are asking and seeing a difference in her. She tells them Jesus is changing everything. She no longer is defined by her pain or circumstance. She is defined by being a child of God, a child that is so greatly loved. That is it. That is the only definition she sees as truth now. She sees herself through the eyes of Jesus. She tries to use every day for good. She uses every moment of pain as a chance to lean on Jesus. She uses her pain as a chance to become stronger. Sometimes, it is just too much for her body and she takes days to recover and finds herself crying out to Jesus as the only strength she can find. On the days that she cannot walk, she listens to His voice in the quietness of being alone with Him. She sees the light and knows she might only find relief when she gets to see Jesus. She just keeps moving forward. She will live victorious over the life that she has been dealt. She doesn't need answers anymore; she needs a Savior to help her walk.

It's when she finally looks back that she can finally see she was being carried when she couldn't stand. She was out in that sea, and when she saw Jesus, she swam father away. Until one day, she heard Him say He loved her and she turned around for just one split second and saw His eyes crying for her to come home. She finally felt His love and swam to Him. The waves might hit her harder than most, but she now holds the hand of the One who can give her true rest, and she will never let go. She is no longer drowning in water just an inch above her nose. She will even help spread the truth to a few people while she's out there with Him. She lives in the truth of who she was created to be, a woman free not from pain, but free from the chains of that pain. The truth is that Jesus changes everything. He changes how you view Him. He changes how you view your circumstance. He changes how you view your pain. If you let Him, even just slowly at first, He will show you His love. You might even be sitting in a church pew every week mad at the Lord for all this pain. She did. She sat there for years and never knew how much He loved her. Every time she listened to a sermon, she thought, "Well, He loves everyone else in this room but not me. I have the pain to prove it." Take out your earplugs put in place by the enemy and hear the voice of God telling you how much you are loved. Listen to Him telling you that there is so much more to life than this, so much more than the past, and so much more than the here and now. Listen to me! You are so greatly loved despite all you see and hear around you! He changed her life when she heard Him tell her she was so very loved. He didn't change her circumstance; He changed her heart. I know this may sound too good to be true. I live in the world's reality. But I also live in the reality of the power of Jesus. And when someone makes the real, raw choice to allow Jesus to move freely in their hearts and minds, there is absolutely nothing that can stop His hope, peace and joy from changing everything about them. It literally overtakes people at the very moment they decide they need a Savior. When someone hears lies for so long and then suddenly hear the truth from God, their soul knows the difference. That wisdom changes everything in one single moment.

Pain Changes Everything

When I look around and see awful things happening, it crushes my soul. The world that God created was perfect and free from sin and people making bad choices. Then sin and evil came into the picture and changed the course of the world. In the same manner that God gives us the ability to choose Him, He also gives everyone the ability to make their own good or bad choices. When your son or daughter makes a bad choice, do you instantly blame God for their bad choice? No, that would be ridiculous. In the same way, when someone makes a choice that is horrible and affects many, we cry out to God and ask why He allowed it to happen? It's natural to want to know the why. But just as you are tempted, so are others. People make bad choices every single day. Sometimes, those choices affect no one but themselves and other times they affect a whole home, a city, an entire group of people, or a whole nation. I do not try to find words that sugarcoat the awful. I have no words to make it okay. I have no words to explain why my brother in law died at twenty-eight years young. I have no words to tell my daughter why God allowed cancer to take her Gigi. I had no words for my friends as they held their newborn babies in a hospital room as they passed away. No one can tell me why my grandmother, the strongest Christian woman I have ever known, cannot even remember all her family members. I can't tell my friend why her mom and dad abandoned her. I have no words for my friends that have waited for years and years to have a child of their own. I can't even wrap my brain around what to say to my friend that was sexually abused. My friend is locked in his brain every single day, seeing, hearing, and feeling the effects of the war he walked through years ago. Nothing I can say will make that better. I don't know what to say to my friend that suffers from a crippling disease. I have a friend whose father chooses alcohol over her and her family every single day. I cannot possibly say something that would make that pain better. These pains are real. These are pains that bring tears to the eyes of every single person who experiences them. I have no words to tell you why bad things have happened to you and me. I can only tell you this: He will use these terrible pains from this earth and make something good. I am not yelling this truth to you from this mountain looking down on your suffering. I am telling you that from the darkest valley, I was also in. The worst thing that has ever happened is that the blameless son of God was crucified on a cross for all of humanity. What happened after this? God threw open the gates of heaven so that all that choose His Son could enter. Maybe you will never know the reason for this pain, but the definition of why doesn't define who He is and it doesn't define who you are either. Write a new definition for yourself. You are loved, cherished, and bought with a price. You, above all, are His most loved. Let Him lead you out of the hurt. Let Him lead you to change. Let Him allow you to see your purpose.

We have to allow Him to change the way we process this life and the things that come our way. We have to change the way we view our pain. We cannot think that because we choose to live with the Lord in control; it means that we will suddenly be exempt from pain. Our lives will now be perfect examples of what it means to follow Jesus! What a lie this is, forwarded by the enemy so that when we do have pain, we lash out at God because we believed the deception that we were exempt from pain. Some of us have lived with deception for so long that we really don't know the Lord can be with us through the pain. I have walked and talked with Christian women who have followed Jesus for over forty years that still struggle with the realization that there might be pain for them. Since you follow Jesus as your Savior, if you believe everything He says with your very own heart, you are set apart from the rest of the world. "See what great love the Father has lavished on us, that we should be called children of God! And that is what we are! The reason the world does not know us is that it did not know him" (1 John 3:1). You are a child of the One, true God! In the midst of great pain, do not let Satan tell you otherwise.

There is something in your life that is proof of the promise that He will be with you in pain. Is it the story of a friend that you never believed? Is it someone that has joy through pain that you never understood? Making it through to another day is sometimes all the proof someone needs that God has a plan for them. Some would say just being able to put one foot in front of the other was proof. Some would say that looking back on their life was proof they had never seen before that the Lord loves them. I have looked back and seen parts of my life that I thought were not fair, just plain not fair, downright, flat-out, call-it-what-it-is not fair. I see it was then that the Lord was carrying me. He did not leave me alone, but the enemy would try to convince me otherwise. He would try to convince me that the Lord left me all alone when something awful happened. He would try to get me to live cold and calloused to the world, bitter and angry that life happened to me the way it did. He would want me to be mad and resentful toward God that didn't make it stop before it started! I know the truth now. "The Lord himself goes before you and will be with you; He will never leave you nor forsake you. Do not be afraid; do not be discouraged" (Deuteronomy 31:8). Soak up those words as you sit there all alone right now. Soak up those words of truth to combat all the lies you have been told for so long. Read that promise over and over. Put it on a sticky note and place it everywhere you look. Read it every day. If you have chosen Him, He will never leave you nor forsake you. Make sure you feel it in your soul. Make certain you want to see and feel the truth. Do you want to see and feel different or have you been chained to negativity for so long you're too comfortable to move? If you even think for a second that you were created for more than this, then get up, put your gloves on, and fight the one that has kept you in this corner since your hurt! Learn to walk with Him through the pain. Learn to see Him in your hurt. There is more to your story, I assure you. There is more than this pain. You are more than this! You were created for more than laying six feet under one day. Trust Him to know what He is doing, because it is *so* much bigger than you can even imagine. But be aware; you will end with freedom from the chains of your circumstance! How would you live with that kind of freedom? Who would you be? Take the hand of Jesus and find out.

Chapter 9

I Am Strong Enough to Forgive Everyone, Including Myself

HAVE YOU EVER BEEN so hurt that it changes you? Meaning that it makes you look at yourself differently? It changes the way you see people. It changes the way you look at the world around you. I'm sure we've all been here, and if you haven't yet, you will probably be at some point. My great moment of change was spurred by a lie, just one single lie, out of the mouth of someone that I loved and trusted immensely. This lie was not a small lie. It was enormous. This lie affected many people and many families. This lie had a lot of branches coming from it. Many other lies had to be told to maintain the first lie. When I found out about the lie, I was so shaken and so hurt I did not know how to move. My brain was literally a jumbled mess trying to see it clearly. My mouth couldn't form words. My mind couldn't form a thought. I instantly became so mad. I had said prayers and cried for this person! I had begged others to pray! In my anger, I called out to the Lord and asked Him what I should do. He immediately asked me to forgive. "So fast? Like, right now you want me to do that?" I told Him that I didn't know how I would forgive! How in the world could I forgive someone who told a lie this tremendous? How could I forgive someone that told a lie that would detriment people if they found out it was indeed all a lie? Maybe someone told her lying was the best way? Maybe someone told her the truth was just too awful to tell? Maybe Satan did a pretty dance around the lie and made it appealing? Perhaps not one person who was involved thought to not be part of this lie. I wonder if she would have had people around her that said they would not support this lie, would she still have told it? I wonder if part of her wants the truth to be told just to set her free.

What Is Forgiveness, Really?

When the Lord asked me to forgive this person and move on, I honestly did not even know where to start. I began at the lie and then moved backward. What should I see through all of this? The longer I searched, the less I found. I realized that it is not my duty to understand the lie. Besides, even if I did uncover why the lie was even told, would it make it any less awful? Definitely not. What I did find when searching was what the meaning of forgiveness really was. After all, if I was going to truly forgive, I had to know what it really meant. I was struggling in a way that I had never struggled before. Not wanting to spread anymore lies, I vaguely told others about the situation and asked them what they would do. They told me that, yes, I had to forgive her, but it was all in my own time. I was shocked when some said I would be able to carry around bitterness if I wanted because I was hurt. Now I was confused. If this was actually the rationale of some Christian people on forgiveness, what then really was the point? Why are we "forgiving" people if we just hold on to all the pain? If we are just going to continue to harbor anger in us, then what is the point of forgiveness? To say I forgave her through my clenched teeth? That cannot be the point. I knew that wasn't the point!

I realized that if I wanted real truth, I would have to ask the people that have heard hard truth from others and the Lord themselves. I would have to seek out the people the Lord put in place to guide me on my journey and direct me one step closer to Him. I could not seek out only those that I knew would tell me what I wanted to hear. As I slowly began to investigate the meaning of true forgiveness through trusted, older, wiser lovers of Jesus and the Lord Himself, I began to see how false that first attitude of forgiveness really was. I found that *true* forgiveness would purify myself and my heart toward the offender. I had asked people who I had walked closely with for a long time how they came to forgiveness through tragedy. What did they do? Many of these people had walked through the unthinkable and forgiven. At the beginning of one person's journey, they asked the Lord why forgiveness was even necessary. Something horrific had happened to them and their offender was long gone. What was the need to forgive that person? The truth, they learned, was that a lack of forgiveness came between them and God. Forgiveness was between them and God and had nothing to do with the offender. Forgiving others was commanded by God for them in their situation and also for me in mine. "For if you forgive men when they sin against you, your heavenly Father will also forgive you. But if you do not forgive men their sins, your Father will not forgive your sins" (Matthew 6:14–15).

I could not pick and choose what in the Bible I wanted to use. If I believed that the Bible was truth, then I also had to heed *all* the commands that are in it, not just choosing what commandments I wanted to follow. I could feel my own lack of forgiveness was standing in between God and myself. "Surely the arm of the Lord is not too short to save, or His ear too dull to hear. But your iniquities have separated you from your God; your sins have hidden His face from you, so that He will not hear" (Isaiah 59:1–2). I did not want *anything* standing in between myself and the Lord. I realized that if I did not know these truths about forgiveness, the enemy could tell me all day long it was not necessary to forgive others and I would so easily have walked into that trap and remained there forever. It was necessary to forgive everyone, not just because it would help me sleep at night but because God forgives me and I have to do the same if I follow Him.

After these people all worked through that first big step of forgiveness, the Lord asked them all to maintain an attitude of forgiveness, every one of them. Meaning He taught them how to be ready to forgive everyone immediately, just as He did. This attitude of forgiveness allowed them to never be caught in the snare of the chains of anger, resentment or bitterness toward someone that they had not forgiven. When an offense was done to them, they forgave. That is the power of God in the life of His follower.

The Truth of the Matter

One thing I realized while talking to all these people about forgiveness was that the offender in all the situations had no idea they were forgiven. The situations that we spoke about were terrible situations that no one should ever have gone through. They were instances in which no other human would condemn the victim for not being able to forgive. These were instances where I couldn't even imagine trying to forgive. But all of these people told me the same thing; forgiveness really had nothing to do with the other person and it had everything to do with them. After all, the offender would go on living whether or not they forgave them. I should be able to offer up forgiveness just like my Father. The definition of forgiveness is the intentional and voluntary process by which a victim undergoes a change in feelings of an offense and is able to let go of negative emotions such as vengefulness, with an increased ability to wish the offender well. Now, when I read that, I thought that there was no way right then that I could wish this person well that lied to me. Furthermore, there was no way that I could just change my feelings about the whole situation no matter how much it stood between myself and the Lord. This is where I would desperately need His help.

After I gathered all my information about forgiveness, I prayed. I just asked that He would allow me to see what He wanted me to see. It was plain and simple. It wasn't complicated. Honestly, I didn't know what to pray. I just asked for the truth. I just wanted to be free from the chains of my hurt feelings. I just wanted to be rid of the emotions that were chaining me down. I was angry, I was sad, and I felt so alone. After all, a lie doesn't just trap the person who first told it; it snares every other person who owns it for even a moment in time. Now I felt all alone because I was in a web of keeping a lie safely hidden. The truth was that Satan wanted to keep me lonely.

He wanted me to think that I was the only one with hurt and pain. He wanted me to live smiling on the outside and hurting deeply on the inside. He wanted me to think that I was all alone. He wanted me to think that no one would understand my betrayal or my suffering. If I would have believed forever that no one understood my pain, I would have been far less inclined to ever discuss forgiveness with anyone. But He told me that there were others that understood and others that had felt deep betrayal. He pointed me to those whom I could speak to. He told me that there was also someone so close to me that understood this completely and with His whole heart. That someone was Jesus, my friend and Savior. His greatest friends, the ones that were chosen to be His friends and disciples, betrayed Him in His darkest hours. He was with me through this pain because He had been here. He had been betrayed. He knew my sorrow and therefore I was not alone. How comforting it was to me to know that He knew my pain and He could walk me through it. In the days and weeks to follow, He revealed truth to me almost daily. In His word, from others I walked with and on Sunday mornings I heard truth.

I came to realize through all of this truth that the actual lie was far less terrible than the truth that it hid. I instantly felt sad for this woman. I could not even imagine the lies that came after this one just to make the first one believable. But at the same time that I was hearing all this truth, I was also hearing lies from my enemy. It was a back and forth game every time I thought about it. I realized I was lied to by not just one, but by many people so as not to expose the first lie. Satan used my feelings against me. "Wow, look how important you were! Everyone lied to you. No one must have thought of you as a friend or that wouldn't have happened. You cannot forgive them. Then they would never be held accountable for this. If the Lord really loved you, He would have kept that hurt from you. He wouldn't have allowed this to happen! You should just wash your hands of them and move on." But then, a whisper, "Kristin." It was Him. I knew because I knew the way He said my name. No one else said it like He did. "I love her just like I love you. Forgive her so she will see how I will forgive her." I was a sobbing mess. It hit me: the enemy weaseled his way into my forgiveness and I didn't even know it was him! I said I wanted nothing to come between myself and this forgiveness and He waged war on that immediately. He was a cunning liar. There was no truth in Him. He enticed me with all I wanted to hear about not having to forgive and was leading me down a path of destruction and judgment. I was so judgmental! I was so calloused. I was so high and mighty. I was so hypocritical! I tell people all the time to forgive, but when that ball was in my court, I threw it back!

Standing next to the counter in my kitchen, I laid my heavy hands down, bowed my head, and began to cry. The tears just wouldn't stop as they ran down my red cheeks and hit the floor. I was so sad for the woman that lied to me. I was so overcome with love for her. I was scared for her future. I wished she could see the Lord. I wished she could see how much He loves her. I wished she could see how much I loved her despite everything. I hated sin then, I hate it now. I hate it in my life and the lives of others. I hate how it tears us away from the Father and the people that really, truly love us. I hate the separation it causes across the lines of family and friends. I hate that Satan sugarcoated his deception and enticed her to a life without the Lord leading her in truth. I hate that he led her to a black hole and took away her ladder. I don't want her to live there. My heart cried uncontrollably for her. In that instant, I forgave her and everyone else that was a part of the lie. I pray for her every day. I want her so badly to see that He loves her. I can only imagine the things that she is living in each and every single day. I want her to see how much she is loved. I want her to see that she is not alone even though I know she feels trapped. She has deserted herself from so many in hopes that her lie will stay contained. She lives every day chained to the lie. Satan wants to make sure she never gets up and out of that hole because he knows who she was before this and who she could be. She was victorious. She was dangerous for God. When she got up in the morning, the enemy knew he was in for a fight. She is now an example to me that I have a choice every single day. I am never above the schemes of the enemy. I am never above being brought down. I have to hitch myself to the Lord every day because the one day that I don't, the enemy's lies will sound a lot like truth. I hope our paths will cross someday and she will know how much I love her despite it all. I hope then she will know how much her Father loves her despite it all. She will know that her sin is not too big for the blood of Jesus to cover.

What Does Forgiveness Literally Look Like?

I reflected as I worked through what had happened in the months after this. I wanted to learn from this. What was He trying to show me? As I was in the midst of trying to learn what all this meant, I was shown something unusual. I was standing on a train station platform. It was cold and the wind was biting my ears and my nose. I was in a puffy winter coat that came all the way up my neck. I don't know what I was waiting for and I don't know how I got there. I looked around to see if I could find someone else, nope, just me, all alone. The train that was approaching was coming fast while blowing the whistle. I watched it come around the corner. I saw the ferocious slatted pilot deflecting the icy cold and eating up the tracks as it got closer. I jolted when the horn blew again. It hurt my ears and I cringed. As it approached, I saw the driver coming into view. I knew in that instant the driver was my enemy. My palms were getting sweaty, my heart rate skyrocketed, and my chest was rising and falling faster and faster. As he drove, he never took his eyes off me. He didn't look like a "devil." He didn't have horns or a tail. There was no fire around him. He wasn't the imaginary figure in a book illustrated by fiery breath and horns. He looked like a man as normal as could be except as he rolled by, way up high in the engineer's seat, my eyes caught a glimpse of his eyes. They were blacker than the darkest night. They had no hope, no love, and no joy. He despised me. If he could have hit me with that train, I knew he would have. I cannot explain the hate that I felt in him when he looked at me. I shuddered and turned away as I shook off the blackness.

As the cars gained speed and whizzed by, I began to look at them. I just instantly knew what was in all of these train cars: sin, stacked high and loaded down in the cars it careened by me. I knew that some of these train cars were mine and some cars belonged to others. As he rolled the cars of sin past my eyes, it seemed as though my cars were not near as full as all the others. Other people had dirty cars and they were filled to the brim with sin. My cars were somewhat good looking and I saw nothing billowing out of the top of them. I began to relax as I thought about how much better I was than everyone else. I quit looking at my cars and began to focus on everyone else's. Their cars were awful! Oh my, how glad I was that my sin was not as ugly as theirs! My breathing slowed and my heart rate was falling. "Whew! Dodged a guilty bullet there!" I thought.

Just then, a prod in my heart. Wait, something was off. I remembered who was driving this train. He *did not* do anything to make me feel better, of that I was sure. But I *was* feeling better watching this train. I felt a hint of deception. This was wrong; it was all wrong. Something was really wrong here. I realized in that second that as long as he was in control of what my sin looked like, I would never see it for what it was. He distorts the view of my sin in a way that made it nonexistent when I saw it the way he wanted me to see it. He distorts sin in a way that makes it invisible to my human eye when reflected. This is why the psalmist says, "Search me, God, and know my heart; test me and know my anxious thoughts. See if there is any offensive way in me, and lead me in the way everlasting" (Psalm 139:23–24). It was utterly important that at all times I was asking the Lord to search me. He was the truth in the search. It was vitally important that I did not hit the point where I unknowingly trusted the enemy to show me my sin. I cannot always see my own sin for what it is; the Lord has to be allowed to show me what the truth of my sin really was.

My Sin, Gone Like a Vapor

As I stood there on that platform, I felt someone next to me but didn't hear anyone coming up, so I turned. It was the Lord. I had no idea where He came from. As soon as He showed up next to me on that platform, He motioned with His eyes for me to look at the cars again. I looked back at the train. In that second, my view of what I was seeing became completely different. My cars were just as dirty as theirs. Some of my cars were actually filled with more sin than other cars! My cars now looked nothing like what I first saw when my enemy showed them to me. Now that I saw my cars for what they were, I didn't have a second to look at anyone else's. With tears of shame in my eyes, I turned to look at Him. I felt the love He had for me radiating from Him. He was not showing me all this to condemn me. He was not showing me all this to make me cower before Him in shame. He was showing me all this so that I could see all that stands in between us. I was seeing all this so that I could see the truth. Right there on that platform, I asked Him to forgive me. I fell on my knees when He opened my eyes. I whispered I was so sorry. I was sorry I sinned and sorry I believed the deception that my sin was pretty. I was sorry I compared my sin to others' sin instead of comparing it to His righteousness. He took my hand and I stood up. I looked at the train. My cars were going up like smoke never to be seen again. He was forgiving me and my sins were disappearing. They weren't going somewhere else to be stored up for later; they were gone like a vapor. The shame and guilt that linked those cars together were now gone as well. The loneliness that those sins caused was gone.

Immediately, there were others all around me on the platform. They didn't walk in; they just showed up instantly. I saw them standing there watching their cars go by. I saw their shoulders sink at the feeling of defeat and shame the enemy heaped onto them. I saw some smiling and looking at others with judgment. I knew they had seen deception in the form of their good-looking train cars of sin, pretty and far less full than everyone else's allowing them to live in ignorant bliss, blinded by the enemy, same story as mine! Some saw their cars so heaping full and awful that they were convinced it was too much for the Lord to forgive and they would remain there, lonely and overcome forever. When the Lord came and stood by me and opened my eyes to His truth, I was finally able to see exactly what He saw, His child whom He died to save, in need of His truth and forgiveness. I was created to be strong enough to forgive and so were you. That strength lays inside of us. We just have to ask Him to help us find the strength.

It Is Not Always an Easy Road

We sometimes get hung up on the fact, "For all have sinned and fall short of the glory of God" (Romans 3:23). All of us have sinned. We all fall short. Our duty is to forgive because He first forgave us. Here is a side note: this does not mean that just because we all sin, we should condone or excuse the behavior of others as simply a "sin." "Well, they sinned and so do I and that's okay." Wrong is wrong no matter how many people do it. If the Lord will forgive them, then we should also. It might take a while, and we might have *a lot* to work through, but we will try because He first forgave us. He gives us many routes to forgiveness. He could allow us to see how hurt another person is, thus making us able to forgive. He could allow us to see their pain. He could allow us to remember the same behavior in ourselves. He could tell us that it is not our place to judge their behavior; it is our place to forgive. He could tell us that we might never understand the evil that we experienced. He could tell us that we will never get an explanation for the "why" this side of heaven. We might have gone through something so horrific that there is no way to explain the behavior, or break it down, or see a bright side. Sometimes, there is no way to sugarcoat what has happened to us. It has made us completely different human beings.

I personally know women that have suffered terrible sexual, physical, and emotional abuse and have come to know peace beyond all understanding through forgiveness. I have known people that have done awful, terrible things themselves, but through forgiveness from the Father, they were able to forgive themselves. It might seem so far off right now. It might seem unimaginable to forgive, but I can assure you that you are not alone in this. The first time that you seek out our Savior's truth in your story, you will begin to change as you finally walk in the direction of forgiveness.

The Snares of the Enemy

Although forgiveness is so easy for our Father, it is frequently the most difficult for us. In a very twisted way, the enemy convinces us that if we forgive, we are allowing the other person "off the hook." I have been in this trap so many times myself! How many times have I wanted to see the repercussions of someone's actions come back to bite them? How many times did I think that my lack of forgiveness was keeping them up at night? I believed that if I did not forgive, I was winning! It is an embarrassing and immature way of thinking. Our enemy is so cunning and deceitful that we actually begin to believe that what he tells us is truth. We define ourselves for so long by hurt in our hearts that it's like having to become a new person when we let it go.

Change is scary. I am the first to tell you that staying where you are might be easier than taking a step out. Forgiveness is that first step out of wherever you are. Showing the love that was shown to you is the first step. "Be kind and compassionate to one another, forgiving each other, just as in Christ God forgave you" (Ephesians 4:32). When He talks about forgiveness, He never says you should only forgive because they ask for it. He never says you should only forgive if they act sorry. He never says you should only forgive if they're nice to you. He doesn't say that forgiveness depends on how big or small the offense was. It's plain and simple; we do not want to forgive. We want to win everything, and we feel forgiveness is tapping out. There is no better case for the refusal of forgiveness than the fact that in no way, shape, or form does the other person deserve it. I would ask what have you done that you deserve forgiveness from your Father? What have you done in your own life that built a bridge to the Father like His death did? You and I do not deserve the forgiveness that is offered to us. We do not. Yet blood was shed for you and me so that we could be forgiven. Forgiveness for us from the Father is so fast that we take it for granted. He does not deliberate on whether or not we should be forgiven. He does not tell us that He'll get back to us in a few days or years with an answer. He does not sit and ponder all the things we have done wrong and see if we are deserving of forgiveness. He does not go to others and ask them if they think we deserve forgiveness. He just forgives us, just in the way we should forgive others. But it is not our choice to forgive or not. We are *commanded* to forgive everyone and there are consequences if we do not. We have this mentality that we can choose not to forgive someone and that is our prerogative, but that is a lie. God loves us unconditionally no matter what we do or don't do, but He is a holy God and that means that He disciplines and corrects His children for not doing what He commands. "My son, do not despise the Lord's discipline, and do not resent his rebuke, because the Lord disciplines those he loves, as a father the son he delights in" (Proverbs 3:11–12).

Forgiveness Unlocks Us All

What if you could have the pleasure of speaking about forgiveness to someone that did not live a life anything like yours? I say pleasure because what an experience it can be speaking with others who are not exactly the same as yourself! I was once in a situation like this. The other person did not know the Lord from a very early age like I had. I never realized how different our mentalities would be. After all, we are both followers of the same Jesus, right? As we got to talking about different things about the Lord, we got on the subject of forgiveness. She asked me what forgiveness meant to me. I sat there in a bewildered sort of way. I had never thought about what it meant to me, to be honest. I had just always known that He would forgive me. This did not mean that I just did whatever I wanted and then asked for forgiveness, but it meant that I knew that when I sinned, if I asked and repented, then I would be forgiven. Forgiveness for me was always there I guess. It was something that was threaded into the way I pictured God.

She smiled at me, the kind of smile that told me she felt sorry for me. She said that my answer sounded like a wonderful answer. "It was a rainbow and sunshine kind of answer." I sat back sort of bewildered. Regardless, it was my truth. She turned, folded her hands, and looked out into space recalling her life behind her. She said she had an awful past, a past that I wouldn't even begin to believe. Her life had been filled with bad choices leading to terrible choices that led her to the cliff of death. Her family held onto her by threads. Her true friends were long gone through all the bad choices. One more wrong choice and she would fall off the cliff. She was on the ledge filled with condemnation and guilt and so very alone from the choices that she had made. Someone then came and met her on that cliff. They were not scared to meet her in her darkest. They didn't shy away because she was too bad. They didn't stay inside the church walls and call out to "all the lost and hopeless." They got up out of their pew, put on their working clothes, grabbed the hand of Jesus, and went out and took Him to her. They weren't embarrassed of her because she made so many bad choices; they made bad choices too. They walked right up to her on that cliff and told her they knew someone who would forgive all her wrong. They knew someone that would also meet her on this cliff and walk her down to solid ground. They knew someone that loved her more than she could imagine despite all the choices. She was introduced to Jesus that day. He didn't care what she had done. He didn't care how many bad choices she had made. He didn't care that she had an awful past. He died on a cross for her and He had a plan for the rest of her life!

It took her a while to process this Jesus. It took her a while to accept His truths. She had listened to the enemy for so long. If she would ask for forgiveness, He would wipe it all away and they could move on. But what about all the hurt she caused? What about her children that didn't trust her anymore? What about every single bridge that she had burned along this way? They told her that the Lord would work all of that out. The Lord would soften hearts and build trust. The Lord would make a way when there didn't seem to be one. She finally asked one day for forgiveness when she was ready and understood the gravity of what she was asking. She told Him she would try with everything she had in her to not make the same bad choices ever again. She told Him she accepted that He died for *her*. She accepted that He was blameless and died on a cross so that this sin, her sin, would not separate her forever from God. She accepted that He loved her. She wanted to live the rest of her life following Him. He forgave her, just like that. She knew He did because her shoulders literally felt lighter. She had a tangible hope for the next years. She could taste it. She knew that she would need His help. She knew the enemy was waiting to take her down. She wouldn't go down without a fight now. She was all alone except for Him. She felt hope in the Lord because He knew exactly where she was going. He didn't care what she had done. She knows He doesn't even think about her sin now, not since that moment she asked Him to forgive her. She doesn't know anyone else who doesn't remember her sin. Everyone but Him remembers everything. If she would stand trial for all the things she had done, Jesus would be the only one in the courtroom who didn't remember her past. She decided that instead of telling them all, she would show them. She would live the life she always wanted to live. She would surround herself now with only the people the Lord wanted around her, people to lift her up and strengthen her, people to pray for her and hold her accountable. She would be the person she always wanted to be. Forgiveness for her means that she can get up every morning and have hope for the day. Forgiveness for her means she doesn't have to live in her terrible, awful past. Forgiveness for her means freedom from the chains that Satan wanted her to live in forever. Forgiveness for her means she has a conqueror. Forgiveness for her means that above all else she is so very loved. This is a real, true and amazing story of forgiveness. I know this because the woman in this story is a part of my story. I held her hands as she said the words out-loud that her heart had yearned to say since learning of Jesus and the Cross. "Yes, I believe that Jesus died for my sins and yes, I believe that His blood was enough to forgive me," she said with shaking hands and tears flowing out of her eyes. "I want to follow Christ, I love Him so much," and she sobbed at an altar where she kneeled before her Savior. I know forgiveness literally changes people. It is real and unlocks even the oldest, hardest hearts.

Walking in Truth

You just have to walk. Sounds funny, right? You just have to keep walking forward. Every time a lie about your shame or a feeling of condemnation or guilt comes to your mind, you have to ask the Lord to take it away and just keep walking with Him. Even after forgiveness, the thoughts of shame might still come because as long as you live, you will have an enemy. The thoughts that you will never be good enough might still enter your mind. The thoughts that God might not have really forgiven you after all might make you stop for a second. But you have to keep going despite it all. You have to keep moving closer to Him. You have to be an overcomer. You have to dodge those lies with truths from His word. You cannot allow them to stick to your soul. It should make you angry that the enemy kept you chained for so long. It should make you never want to ever be there again. It even makes *me* angry that the enemy was so cunning and successful on my own path to forgiveness. I let that anger fuel me to never let him chain me again. I let that fuel me to help everyone else out of those chains. Even to this day, my enemy tries to sneak in and remind me of things that I have done. It is in those moments that I remind him and myself that the Lord has forgiven me and I *will not* pick those sins up again.

When you think of all the things in which you have been forgiven, let the Lord remind you that you are so very loved and that He died on a cross for you and your sins. Let the Lord remind you of all of the wonderful things that He has for you. Let the Lord remind you of the things He has in store for your future. Let the Lord remind you that He doesn't think about your sin. Tell your enemy that the Lord says this about your sin: "As far as the east is from the west, so far has he removed our transgressions from us" (Psalm 103:12). Let the Lord remind you that you're a new creation. Learn to rest in Him. When you feel overwhelmed and you feel like picking up the past again, you stop right where you are and do not pick it up. Refuse to pick it up. Right then and there in that moment, let the Lord be bigger than your past, your hurt, and your scars. Walk in His light and see all those cars filled with sin go up in smoke, never to be seen again, *never to be seen by Him again.*

Chapter 10

I Am Strong Enough to Be Uncomfortable

I WAS RECENTLY IN A discussion with someone and they asked me if I felt like my walk with the Lord was "good enough." Good enough for who? For myself? For God? For my pastor? I said "yes." I felt like my walk was good enough for myself in the place I was. We proceeded to discuss who it was that should be defining my "good enough" walk. Should my walk with Him ever feel "good enough"? Is there a point in time where I have done all I can do in my walk with Christ? Had I come to a point that I was okay with being a slave to spiritual mediocrity? Before this simple conversation with an honest friend, I had been unknowingly convinced that it was okay that my walk with Jesus had come to a standstill. I wasn't going backward, but that's the part where I was deceived. I was convinced that since I wasn't "backsliding" in my faith that I was fine just where I was. No need to fix something that wasn't broken, right? Why would I take a step out of my Christian comfort zone? I can hear myself saying, "It's so easy here. I'm happy here. Doesn't the Lord want me to be comfortable? I wouldn't be comfortable if I had to move from this place." I told my friend sitting across from me that I knew the Lord would want me to be comfortable. She stared at me for a second, looked around, took a big gulp of air, and then told me that, "No, the Lord did not exist to make me comfortable." He did not die on a cross so that I would be comfortable all the days of my life. He wanted me to have joy in all I do. He wanted me to have joy when life is rough and when it was "good." He wanted me to take joy in the blessings and in the pain. He wanted me to have joy in my sometimes-uncomfortable walk with Him no matter where He takes me. There will be points, she told me, when I would have joy but not necessarily be happy. This life wasn't about coming to the next thing that would make me happy; it was about walking with Jesus wherever *He* wanted to go and wherever *He* leads. There will be mountains of joyfulness and valleys of sadness. But, in the midst of it all, I could have joy because I knew that He was walking with me and guiding me every step of the way and I was saved! "Though you have not seen him, you love him; and even though you do not see him now, you believe in him and are filled with an inexpressible and glorious joy, for you are receiving the end result of your faith, the salvation of your souls" (1 Peter 1:8–9). How great a joy that this promise produces!

Mediocrity at Its Finest

"C'mon Kristin," you say to me now. "Really, how long can we keep praying, and going to church, and doing good 'Christian things' without getting burned out? How long can we keep doing all these things without it becoming just what we do?" If we are not careful, all of our good work turns into something that we are not doing for Him anymore, but something we do out of ritual. We go to church because it's Sunday. We volunteer at church because that's what church members do. We say things like "God is good all the time, He has a plan for you, just trust in Him, I'm praying for you, and He loves you!" We've said it and heard it enough that we don't even think about what it means anymore. Sitting there that day talking with my friend, I realized that it was okay with me that I was not moved anymore by the Holy Spirit. I was so comfortable where I was at. Everything in life seemed to be going good and I was comfortable in that spot. I was comfortable at my church on Sundays. I was comfortable with my kids and my career and my husband. This was how everyone's walk goes, right? It was okay with me that I just felt mediocre. Life was not amazing for me, but I *was comfortable.* I knew all of what the Lord told me to do. I knew the ways that He called me to speak. I knew the ways He called me to love others. *But when was the last time that I acted to others like I really knew all of that?* When was the last time I took a step out of my row at church to be used by God as a member of the body of Christ? By being mediocre in my faith, I turned into someone that was okay with sitting on the sidelines of walking with Christ doing "just enough to get by." When was the last time that I was uncomfortable for God?

How was I so duped into believing that my spiritual mediocrity was okay? I see now that my fire that Christ lit inside my heart when I accepted Him was now only a dim flame. My praise was merely uttered words. My prayers were the same and only before every meal. I was a mediocre Christian. There, I said it. It's the truth. It's like a really long lunch break I couldn't come back from. It's like a nap I just couldn't wake up from. This was not all there to life as a follower of Jesus. I didn't see any of this until someone spoke what was on their heart about me. I know that woman was talking to Jesus before she came and met me and delivered a one-two punch of truth. I realized that people would not be attracted to the words that I would say; they would be attracted to the light that I would display. What was the light that I was displaying? Was I even displaying one at all?

Making That Fire *Blaze*

I went through periods where my fire was just a small flame and periods where it burned brightly. I realized that for a very long time, it was just a minimal flame, not even enough to roast a marshmallow. Satan did not want to see my fire raging. He did not want my fire to be burning so hot that I couldn't contain myself from telling everyone about Jesus. He fought with everything he had to make sure I did not move from where I was. He wanted me to remain chained to mediocrity inside God's church. He would do everything He could possibly do to convince me that what I was doing was good enough. He lived every single day to make sure that I was making myself happy in whatever way I could. He would use every cunning, deceitful tactic to make me stay at the same spiritual place I had been for the last five years. He didn't want me to take a closer step to Christ, and as sure as the sun rises each morning, he definitely didn't want my fire to spread.

What a tragedy a weak flame in my heart was to Jesus. Being comfortable was not hard. Being comfortable would never make me move. I don't know about you, but being comfortable never spurred any change for me. If I never walk out of my comfort and into the unknown with Jesus, how would I know how much power He possesses? How would I have learned to trust Him if I never held His hand out into the waves? Are you standing at the edge of the sea, comfortable on the bank? Is He asking you to take His hand and walk through the waves with Him? It will be uncomfortable, I promise you. Great things wait for you in the sea when you go out with Him. Will you trust Him to lead you through the uncomfortable? Are you strong enough to take His hand and walk through it? Let Him teach you about His power and might. You *are* strong enough to take His hand and walk through the uncomfortable maybe to a place that you have never been before. Great joy waits for you not only in the destination of His will, but in the journey. Your fire will rage once you get out of your "comfortable place." You will begin to feel yourself desiring Him more and more when you leap out into the sea, into the arms of the One who wants to show you great joy and passion for doing His sometimes-uncomfortable work.

Section 3

Kind: Having or Showing a Friendly, Generous, and Considerate Nature

Chapter 11

I Am Kind, Even with a Broken Heart

WHILE IN THE MIDDLE of writing this book, my grand-mother Dorothy, whom I dedicated this book to, passed away. To say that I had to write in the middle of heartbreak is a vast understatement. She was the first one that I told about this book and the one I consulted about everything in it thus far. She was my rock, my best friend, and my confidante. I knew she would not get to read this book, the Lord told me that early on. I shared that truth with her and she said, "Well, let's just talk about it now then," and smiled at me. I knew she also knew she wouldn't live to see this book in her hands. When I had about forty pages complete, I took it over to her to let her read it. I wanted to make sure she felt the love of Christ through these pages. I wanted to make sure I was conveying the realities and truths of following Christ. She returned it to me a few days later, and with one breath, she said "It's all very true. Some is very hard to hear, but it's so very true. We are so very loved." I take that with great pride because this woman knew how to love and what it really meant. I sit here with tears streaming down my face knowing how the world was left a better place because of her love and kindness.

I recall one day with her very well. It was a hot Indiana summer day. She was wearing a house coat. It was purple. (I am the proud owner of that housecoat now, and although I have many other robes, I have only one housecoat.) The sun was streaming in her big, old windows in the front room. She was sitting in her recliner as her eyes were recalling the years past. She often went to this place. It must have been happy for her there. It brought her great joy I know. Sometimes when she ventured off into her thoughts, she would smile. I watched her, wondering what she was recalling. She must have felt loved where she went to; her smile told me that. "Grandma, how do you know how to love so good?" I asked her. She came back from wherever she was and looked at me. She stared at my face for a moment like she was looking at me but not really looking at me. She told me she just showed people the kind of love that the Lord showed her. I took it in but didn't really feel it until much later. Is it really that easy? Is there really one type of love that is perfect? It always seemed as though my grandma knew the perfect way to love each and every single person in her life. Everyone in my family would vouch for that statement. Although she loved us all the same amount, and on the same level, she loved us all very differently. I loved her because she made me feel so special to her. I loved her because she was so kind to me. I loved her because she was His truth when I couldn't hear it.

She was so much more than a nice person. Do you know what I mean? There are plenty of "nice people" walking around. They are everywhere. Nice people open the door for you because that's what society expects them to do. There is no deeper level to being nice. Nice people are nice because it is what is expected of them. Kind people see you'll get to the door before them with arms full, so they run ahead to get there before you to open the door. They might even ask to help you carry some stuff and risk making themselves late for helping you. (But they'll never tell you that.) Kindness is rooted in something far deeper. A kind person is kind because of their love for others. See the difference? Kind people are always thinking of others. They don't care about how they are perceived in society; all they care about is others. Have you met someone that is truly kind? Kindness is the quality of being friendly, generous, and considerate. It is going above and beyond just being nice. Kind people go out of their way to love you. They go out of their way to show you compassion. They go out of their way to do things for you that you might not even deserve and they want no recognition for it.

When you come in contact with a truly kind person, they might leave you speechless, scratching your head asking why in the world they would be so kind. They don't even know you! They do all this without wanting anything in return. They do all this without even thinking about it. It swells up from the depths of their fully awakened spirit. It radiates from them. Their kindness permeates every hard surface of the world they come in contact with. Their kindness seeps through the cracks in the walls you have built around your own heart. Their kindness doesn't care who you are, what you look like, what past you have, or what choices you have made. It doesn't care the condition of your heart. It doesn't care if you go to church. It doesn't care if you even care. They have felt the kindness from the Lord when they were at their worst. They felt His kindness when they were least deserving of it. They want to spread it around. They want everyone to feel it. They want everyone to get just a glimmer of the kindness and love the Lord showed to them. It spreads from them to others like electricity going over power lines. It cannot be stopped. It cannot be hindered. Even if someone tries to stop the current of kindness, it will find another way. This was my grandmother. Her current of kindness had no end. She wanted to be like Jesus. She wanted to be like everything that He is. What specifically does the Lord command us to do when we love someone? Does it have to be only older people that have mastered what it means to love? Can there be twenty and thirty something people that show undying love and kindness for everyone around them?

In this age, the word and action of love are thrown around so frequently that we lose the depth of what love really means. I want to love people on the level that my grandma did. I want everyone who I love to *know* that I love them and not just because I tell them I do. If they were asked, "Do you think Kristin loves you?" I want them to be able to say exactly *how* they know I love them. Do you know that Christ loves you? Now tell me how you know that. Do you know that because you feel it in your heart? Do you know that because He has whispered that to you when you needed it most? Do you know that because someone who loves Him showed the same love to you? Do you know that because even though you went through the valley,

He was with you? I know He loves me because He died on a cross for me and forgives my sins. I know He loves me because He asked me to come down off the ledge and taught me to dance again. Christ loves us because we are His children. He loves us even though we do wrong. He loves us even though we don't make the choices He would want us to make. He loves us even though we might not love Him back. My grandmother never asked me how much I loved her. She never asked me how much I cared. She never based the love she put out on how much love I gave her. Recalling her life when I knew her, she had many broken hearts. My grandpa passed away and she lived longer than most all of her friends. Death can be the ultimate heartbreak for a period of time in all of us. But she never treated anyone any differently when her heart was breaking. I can imagine that she had learned some lessons earlier in her life and the way she was with me was a product of all of those lessons. She was never conditional about her love and kindness, and that is not something that she learned from the world.

Kindness in the World Today Now Lies in Ruins Under the Crumbling Towers of Love

We live in a world today where we show people love and kindness on a conditional level. This is bred into our thinking. Our parents might do it, so we do also. Our friends might do it, so we do too. Our church friends might do it, so we follow suit. We show people kindness based on how kind and generous they are to us. We condition our love and kindness based on the love and kindness they show us. My heart has been broken more times than I even want to count. I can imagine that your heart has been broken quite a few times as well. Together, our broken hearts are caused by ourselves, our friends, our enemy, death, suffering, circumstances, and by life itself. It is ironic to me that our broken hearts are the things that we never want to admit but also one of the things in our lives that do the most damage. Think about it: the event that most often leads to any new path in life is most often a broken heart. Sometimes broken hearts lead to positive changes in our lives like new relationships, new dreams, and realized truths. But sometimes the destruction from a broken heart can last over many relationships and years and can even be passed to our children. We would think that with broken hearts being so prevalent, we would talk about them and, yet, we don't. We do not even tell others that they have broken our hearts. Rarely do we ever take our broken hearts to Jesus and ask Him to heal them for us. We look to addictions and pleasures to bring us out of our broken hearts. We might move across town, across state lines, or across the country to get away from our broken hearts, all the while thrusting the brokenness deeper and deeper inside of our souls as we clamor to get away from it. We literally do everything we can think of to do except hand over our hearts to the ultimate healer. Why in the world would we just not hand it over? Why do we allow our broken hearts to cause so much bitterness, callousness, and regret in us? Why do we act like we aren't walking around broken? I have an idea: The enemy veils our broken hearts in shame so that we will never want to discuss it with anyone, especially the Lord. I believe the general consensus among us would be if you are weak enough to get your heart broken, you better be strong enough to not talk about it! And so that is exactly what we do. This is exactly how the enemy makes sure we walk around chained to our broken hearts forever. We lock away our broken hearts and swim farther and farther away from Jesus out in that sea.

Broken Hearts Are Susceptible to Major Attack

When we have a broken heart, there is a serious crack down the middle of it, a deep, real pain that exists in our hearts. This means there is a line of very sensitive heart flesh now being exposed. When our hearts are not broken and the enemy lies to us, we are able to combat the lies because of the tough guard on our hearts. When we have a broken heart, the enemy's lies strike that exposed flesh with a ferocious potency like our hearts have never experienced before. When that exposed flesh is hit with lies, our hearts become inflicted with deceit and untruth. It is hard enough to counter deceit from the enemy when we have a strong, guarded heart; but a weak, unguarded, broken heart is no match for our voracious enemy. He tells us lies like "if your God really loved you, He would have never allowed your heart to be broken" or "I thought you prayed about this, He obviously doesn't care about your prayers." Then as the lies pummel the crack in our hearts, the enemy throws in that crack seeds of bitterness and rage. This is the exact moment when we decide that we do not have to be kind to others because we have a broken heart. We now have inside of us roots of bitterness, rage, slander, and malice directed not just at those who broke our hearts but to everyone that looks at us the wrong way. The things that come out of our broken hearts are exactly the things that broke them in the first place. But how did it get to this point? Who told us that we had the right to mistreat others because our hearts were broken?

The simple truth is that we have to love, no matter what shape our heart is in. Now, before you roll your eyes at me through your broken heart, believe me, there have been many, many times in my life when I did not want to hear that. I did not want to be kind, much less to the person that broke my heart. But I am a follower of Jesus, and if I am who I say I am, I have to love. I have to. There are no if's or but's to it. I am commanded to love and so are you. But the commands don't stop there: we are also commanded to "get rid" of all that exists in our hearts that would defeat the kindness that we are supposed be showing to humanity. But really, when is the last time we listened to His command and ridded our hearts of all negativity?

Ephesians 4:31–32 states, "Get rid of all bitterness, rage and anger, brawling and slander, along with every form of malice. Be kind and compassionate to one another, forgiving each other, just as in Christ God forgave you." It states nowhere in this text that if someone breaks our hearts, we do not have to be kind. No, it says that we have to be kind and compassionate and *forgive* others. It leaves no exceptions. But don't listen to me alone. Don't take my word that this is what it says just because you are reading this book. Go to your Bibles and read it for yourselves. This verse does not say that we are not allowed to have broken hearts, after all, we are human. We will have broken hearts. It does say, however, what we are *not* allowed to hide in our hearts for any reason: bitterness, rage, anger, brawling, slander, and malice. The Lord wants our hearts to be free to just love. He wants our hearts clear so that we can see what He sees in the world. He knows that the things that take up residence in our hearts are the things that ultimately control us whether we would admit it or not. He desires to heal our hearts until only love remains.

But, as simple as it sounds to "just love," we sometimes get lost on how to do it! The first steps are always admission and inventory. We have to acknowledge that our hearts are broken and take an inventory of the negative things that reside in there. Literally, we have to sit down, admit to ourselves that our hearts are broken, and ask the Lord in prayer to tell us what exists in the midst of our hearts that needs to be removed. "Search me, God, and know my heart; test me and know my anxious thoughts. See if there is any offensive way in me, and lead me in the way everlasting" (Psalm 139:23–24). He will bring to the surface all that needs sifted out. We are not allowed to remain angry and bitter. He will, maybe slowly at first, bring to your mind all that needs to be removed from your heart so that you can truly love and be kind. I take an inventory of my heart almost every single day. The Lord brings things to my mind that need to be out of my heart and then I respond by asking Him to remove them and ask for His help to make sure I do not put them back.

Missing the Point

As I look back now, I can clearly see that I was closest to the Lord when my heart was broken. How do I know that? It was simple: I sought Him more. I was hurting and I needed Him every minute of the day. I sought Him because I needed to feel how much I was loved. I sought Him to find a way out of my broken heart. I sought Him to give me the peace that I could find no where other than Him. I sought Him because I wanted to lash out in anger. I wanted to say mean and hurtful things to anyone that I could say them to. I admit it, I fell short. I allowed the enemy to lie to me and tell me that I had the right to project the effects of my broken heart onto the world because my heart was broken and it wasn't fair. But when I was with my Creator in prayer amidst my broken heart, that wasn't what He told me. I was not allowed to mistreat anyone. I was not allowed to not be kind. I was not allowed to not love. At the same moment that I felt this conviction, I also felt relief that He accepted me, broken heart and all. I felt relief that I could tell the Lord how I felt and ask Him to help me work through it. I actually felt relief that someone understood my breaking heart. I honestly felt relief that I could admit the things that I had done in anger and resentment. It was as if getting them "off my chest" to God felt good for me. I was admitting my failures, repenting and trying to move on. I was finally listening to truth and speaking it to myself. "I am loved. I am treasured. I am not allowed to be unkind. I am not allowed to do anything but love. I am commanded to forgive. I am commanded to rid my heart of things that are not good. I follow Jesus and I have to act like it."

What Is the Point?

The greatest definition of being kind with a broken heart comes from Jesus. He died so that we could be righteous and meet Him in heaven someday. He died so that we could walk with Him every day and not just when we needed a way out of a broken heart. He died to save us from our sin. He showed us a level of kindness that can never be compared to anyone ever again. He died on a cross to save a world of people that would hate him. He died for all the people that say He isn't who He says He is. He died on a cross to show people a kind of mercy they have never experienced before. Actually, when He was hanging on the cross, "Jesus said, 'Father, forgive them, for they do not know what they are doing...'" (Luke 23:34). He was talking about those who crucified Him! You think His heart wasn't breaking right then? Thinking of a whole earth of people who wouldn't choose to follow Him? You think His death was an easy choice for Him?

He did not just die for the people who would show Him kindness in return; He died for the people who would hate Him, all to give them the chance to take up their cross and follow Him. He showed kindness to people that don't deserve it, us, all of us, you and me, the people that don't deserve it. I can see His tears as He looks at the people who keep swimming away from Him. This not only is the people who have never chosen to follow Him with their lives but also the people who have and then wandered away. God knows we are human and we will have broken hearts caused by other people and be angry and hurt. Satan wants to lock us up inside our broken hearts and never let us out. He wants us to hang onto the anger and hurt and the despair for the rest of our lives. He does not want us to live free and joyous with Jesus. He knows that if we move from our own personal broken hearts, we might be able to feel what breaks the Lord's heart; he knows that heavenly broken hearts lead to great change and freedom for people. He wants us to hold onto despair until our last days on earth. He wants us to be mad at God forever about our broken hearts. He wants us to be unkind. He likes the cycle. We get a broken heart, we treat people terrible, then he makes us feel shame for acting the way we did. The worst thing about this cycle is that it will never stop until the love of Jesus and His truth put a roadblock in the lies from the enemy. Then and only then will we will be able to see through the shame and into the eyes of a selfless Jesus.

The Sobering Look of a Broken Heart

You might know someone that you can pinpoint that lives daily through a broken heart. You might even be one yourself. I know someone that lives this way. His broken heart has made him difficult to be around and has made him hardened to the world and unwilling to discuss the topic of Jesus. He doesn't recognize that His heart is broken, but it is. This broken heart has led to anger, bitterness, and disgust for all things "church." His heart is broken by watching followers of Jesus. You read that correctly. His heart is broken because in his mind, he never sees "followers of Jesus" actually feeding the poor, and helping the needy, the afflicted, or the sick. He sees us sitting in church pews on Sundays talking about how much we love Jesus and then walking out the doors, telling no one. He sees us making a big deal out of ourselves as we tell anyone who will listen about the "good works" that we have done. He mocks Christ's followers and calls them all hypocritical. He laughs at their "values." As far as he is concerned, he is a "better" human being than most of them; and honestly, he might be. He gives a lot of money away to help the needy and the sick. He spends a lot of time thinking about other things but how he can further his own dreams. He doesn't understand how a God that seems to require so much out of His followers can let them go on for so long never doing anything outside of the church walls to further His kingdom. He doesn't want to serve that God. The enemy has convinced him he wants nothing to do with Jesus because of all he has seen. He doesn't understand how we can say that we follow Jesus when the only time we think of Him is when we say we are "going to heaven someday." He knows a lot about the Bible. He could give a one-two punch to someone that wants to chat about how well they think they know Jesus and what the Bible says about following Him. He wanted to know about Jesus at one point. He was taught about Him. He definitely thinks he has seen Jesus through some people and why wouldn't he think that? If someone says they follow Jesus and then acts and talks in a manner completely different from who He is, what do they expect from the people watching?

In the beginning, before he decided to walk very far away from Jesus, he just sat back and watched His "followers" to see what they were doing. He watched to see what was expected of him if he decided to follow Jesus. He did not take the decision lightly. He wanted to know what He had to do if he devoted his life to this Jesus. I know what you will say here: that he should have looked biblically at what it said to be a follower of Jesus and then decide. You would say that he should not have watched humans because they would fail. Well, I agree with you to an extent, but what about everything biblically that tells followers what to do and how to act? Why would someone that is about to make a decision to follow Jesus not think that they could look at who is following currently and then decide if that is what they want? How many come through the church doors because of an invitation by us, and then sit next to us in their cubicle and listen and watch us to decide if Christ is who they want to also follow? We sometimes say, "Don't watch me follow Jesus. I don't know what I am doing yet." But in reality, what we are really saying is, "Don't watch me follow Jesus because I know what I should be doing and I am choosing not to do it."

After watching and listening to Christ followers, this man decided that he wanted nothing to do with Christ. He saw that He could "accept Jesus as His Savior" and then go on living His life how he always had. He would be getting into heaven after his "salvation," so what was the point to live like a follower of Jesus? In his mind, there was no point. He saw judgmental, non-loving, lukewarm Christians heading the show for Christ and he wanted to get as far away as he could. He saw that their lives would probably be the same exact life if Jesus wasn't in it. So, with his broken heart, he decided to keep living the life he was living without Jesus in it because after all, what was the difference?

This man has lived in his broken heart even to this very day, never even really knowing for himself who this Jesus is! If he ever really did decide to meet Him for himself, He would be the change that he wants to see. He would let no other walk affect his own. He would be one of the people that *want* people to follow their example. He would be one saying to them, "Follow my example, as I follow the example of Christ" (1 Corinthians 11:1). He would see that there are consequences for never taking up their crosses and following Jesus. "I know your deeds, that you are neither cold nor hot. I wish you were either one or the other! So, because you are lukewarm-neither hot nor cold-I am about to spit you out of my mouth" (Revelation 3:15–16). He would see that the Lord commands believers to leave everything behind and *follow* His ways. "Large crowds were traveling with Jesus, and turning to them He said: "If anyone does not hate father and mother, wife and children, brothers and sisters-yes, even their own life-such a person cannot be my disciple. And whoever does not carry their cross and follow me cannot be my disciple"" (Luke 14:25–27). He would see what Jesus's love really looks like when not tainted by the people who say they love Him but act differently. "This is how we know what love is: Jesus Christ laid down his life for us. And we ought to lay down our lives for our brothers and sisters. If anyone has material possessions and sees a brother or sister in need but has no pity on them, how can the love of God be in that person? Dear children, let us not love with words or speech but with actions and in truth" (1 John 3:16–18). He would find that, in fact, when one truly trusts Jesus with their whole heart and begins to follow Him, that is the beginning to a life vastly different than what they had before. They would see, feel, and be aware that Jesus is literally living in them and that makes them *very* different than the person they were before. "I have been crucified with Christ and I no longer live, but Christ lives in me. The life I now live in the body, I live by faith in the Son of God, who loved me and gave himself for me" (Galatians 2:20). This life we now live should set us apart from the world. Well, it *should* anyway.

Being a mediocre Christian is a path to destruction and I have no doubt that it is not okay with Jesus. Our lives should *never* be the reason that someone else decides they have no need to follow Jesus. If we are in fact followers of Jesus, our lives should propel others to know Him. Our lives should never give others a broken heart about what it means to know Jesus. If this man could ever see Jesus for who He really is, and not based on what He sees from His "followers," I have no doubt in my mind that he would be one of those "weird people" desperately in love with Jesus. He would be the one throwing open the church doors and running to take the truth and freedom of Jesus to the poor, the sick, and the lonely. He would be giving all he could to help the cause for Christ. He would be a man that helped so many souls knowing the real Jesus. His broken heart could someday be loosed from its chains. Maybe someday he will come across a person in love with Christ and this stranger can show him the Jesus who can free Him from those chains of his broken heart. Then he can truly live free while running toward Christ. That is what we are supposed to be doing through loving Christ after all, showing others the love that loosed our hearts from the chains that bound it.

We Are All Capable of Kindness Through Brokenness (*All of Us*)

The Lord moved someone in my line of sight out in that water that would teach me what it meant to accept that my heart was broken and move on from that. This woman would come to be one of my most treasured women of God. What I see in her reminds me of Jesus. Her past is pain. Her path is lined with shards from her broken heart.

When I first met her, I was instantly attracted to her joy. I could tell immediately that she was not faking this joy. Her smile was real. As I watched her with her children, I took note of how "motherly" she was. She must have had wonderful parents to show her how to do this! She was so patient with them, so understanding and kind. The enemy instantly told me that we would have nothing in common. After all, I was not this woman. I was reeling from carrying around my broken heart from my own past and couldn't ever find it in myself to be who she was. I listened to the enemy telling me that she was much better than me, so I didn't go up and talk to her. Actually, he made me feel shameful when I was around her because I yelled at my kids and had a quick tongue. My anger got out of hand and hers did not. He told me that she was *obviously* very different from me; she was everything that I should be but was not.

I cannot remember the first time she and I finally talked in great length. I cannot remember what propelled me to go up to her. What did I have to loose after all? I felt a draw to her, but I had no idea why. As it turns out, everything I thought about her was wrong. She was, in fact, broken.

She had come from a broken heart. Her past was not rosy. She learned how to be what she was from Jesus and the people He placed in her life to guide her. I was astonished. She spoke with love about the people that hurt her. She spoke of them as if she felt sorry for them. She felt sorry that they never felt Jesus hold them like she had. She felt sorry for them in that they never desired Him to free them from their broken heart. She cried for them. She wasn't angry that they weren't what she needed. She was sorry that they weren't what

God called them to be, but that was not her cross to bear. Their decisions were made by them, and one day standing before God, she would not be responsible for their decisions. She was joyful that she met a Savior that was everything she needed. She held on to that joy. She had forgiven the ones responsible for her broken heart years ago. She didn't live in the turmoil that a broken heart causes. She had felt for years that if only she was good enough, she would've been loved more. If she had just been smarter, or prettier, she would've been loved more. She spent many, many years in this position. It led to feelings of inadequacy and she let everyone walk all over her. She cowered in the corner with her broken heart at one point in her life before now.

Then she gave everything over to the Lord. She gave over her feelings of not being good enough. She gave over all her fears of never being what she needed to be for everyone. Jesus loved her. He really, really loved her. This was a type of love that she had never experienced. This was a type of love that she felt she didn't deserve. She was in awe of Him. She didn't feel worthy of such a special gift. He taught her that she was a prize. She finally felt truly loved for exactly who she was, in the condition that she was in. She decided that she would never again live in the pieces of her broken heart. She let the Lord stitch it back together with love. She then took that love and showed kindness to the ones who broke her heart in the first place. She is commanded to love even her enemies, so that is exactly what she does. Maybe someday, they will make the choice to follow Jesus. Maybe someday, they will look in the mirror and begin to let Him mend their own broken hearts. She saw the Lord's kindness through her broken heart and was changed. She now will stop at nothing to show others that same kindness spurred from the love of her Father.

The Trap Was Laid Before Us

I missed the whole opportunity with Christ that a broken heart presents: it was supposed to spur me on to change. While it drew me to Him, it was supposed to make me crave being with Him in a way that I would never make the choice again to leave Him. It was supposed to show me that the love that I felt from Him was a love that everyone needed told about. I would love to tell you that because of someone breaking my heart, I turned from my self-centered mentality and began to work for Jesus, but I did not. I was supposed to learn so much from all of my broken hearts. But I never did. I always asked what I needed to see to help my heart but never asked what change He wanted to do with my life through my broken heart. And so, my heart kept being broken and I continued to learn nothing. Believe me, I know it's hard to think of others when your life is crumbling. I know it's hard to see things or others in place of your own thoughts and feelings. But, when we go to the Lord, He brings us to the place where His plan is much bigger than us, a place where our broken hearts could make way for so much good.

It was not until I actually stood out in that water and saw what breaks the Lord's heart that I changed the way I walked with Christ. It was not until my breaking heart was a reflection of His did I change. It was not until I saw all of those people standing out in that water that I moved closer to Christ through my breaking heart. When I saw all of the people, created to be loved by God, out there flailing, gripped with fear, and unable to move out of that place, I began to see things bigger than my broken heart. When I watched the calculated war being waged on souls to rip them from the only true freedom they might ever know, my heart broke in a way that it could not have been broken by a human being. I learned it would remain in this broken state for the rest of my time here on earth. But it was going to serve a purpose now. Each day, that break in my heart for humanity propels me to move forward with Christ with an urgency that I cannot even explain. If I only had 120 years left on earth, that wouldn't be enough time to reach everyone that needs Him. That's why each and every single one of us has to be diligently working every day for Christ, because some cannot reach all, but all can reach some! Not one good speaker can reach all the masses. Not one good book can touch all the hearts. Not one good praise band can make all the hearts sing with joy for the Lord. It takes the army of God to stand tall, take up their armor, and go and preach the gospel to the ends of the earth. It takes an army of God's people, armed with what breaks the Lord's heart and not our own, to reach all the souls that desperately need to know Him and be freed.

You might be out there swimming away from Him. You might be out there thinking that He is not who He says He is. I would ask that you take a good look at where you are. How long have you been here? How long have you lived in this heartache? How long have you been chained to resentment and bitterness? How long have you lacked true kindness because of your broken heart? How long have you carried a "bad attitude" just because your heart said that you could? Did you even know you were here? He loves you greatly. I know that in the deepest part of my soul. It's not just something that I say anymore. I *know* that He loves me. See your chains for what they are today. See your broken heart and what's it's doing to you. See how it makes you interact with others. See the deception the enemy has been telling you. See how long he has had you locked to your hurt. See the responsibility that you have as a child of God! You are responsible to hold yourself to a different standard. You are called to help others. You are called to be kind. (There is no exception!) Hear Him calling you out of the deep waters. See Him sending others to help you. Witness the freedom in others that He has *for you* as well. Start to swim in the direction of your freedom. You were not meant to live chained to this broken heart for all your days on this earth. He will free you. That's what He does. Ask Him and get ready to actively start swimming to Him. Get on your knees, cry out to Jesus, find someone that really knows Him to talk to and start taking steps closer to Him.

After all, you and I were not just meant to go to church on Sundays. We were not meant to just work our whole lives to try to be happy. We were not meant to never see the poor. We were not meant to pass by the suffering and shrug with disregard for them. The enemy has lied to us for far too long. We were created to do Christ's good work. What can you do with your broken heart? Who can you help? What injustice will ignite your heart? We have to use the fuel from our broken hearts for good. We just have no idea how a person with Christ and a broken heart caused by injustice could wreak so much havoc on the enemy's plans to keep people away from Christ and His goodness. We just have no idea how much we *could* help. If we asked the Lord to heal our broken hearts caused by others, if we then asked Him to break our hearts for what breaks His, if we were kind to everyone through our brokenness, and if we allowed ourselves to be *used* by God, He would throw open the floodgates of the plans He has for us.

Chapter 12

I Am Kind Enough to Show Others the Love that Was First Shown to Me

I HAVE MANY EXAMPLES OF kindness from those that know me personally and treat me with kindness. But ask me to tell you a story of kindness that was shown to me by a stranger. I might have to get back to you on that. See, kindness is easy when we know who we are directing it to. Kindness is easily spotted by those that know you as kind. In fact, if you are around people that know you as a kind person, you will continue to be kind. But, when being around others that do not know you as kind, it is easy to treat them uglier than you would if you knew them. Sometimes, when we are around people that have an edge or that we know won't be kind to us, it is then the most difficult to radiate kindness. Kindness is sometimes hard when you don't know how another person will respond. Sometimes, being kind is the hardest when you *know* the other person will not be kind in return.

Exhibiting Kindness in the "Real World"

We have a group at my church that cooks meals for mothers who have just had a baby. Sounds pretty simple, right? Someone puts a mother and her family on the list and bam, food starts being delivered to her home after she returns from the hospital. No one asks if the recipients are members of the church. No one asks if they give money to the church. No one asks if they also volunteer to help the church. I received a meal from one of these women. What she left with me was not just the taste of good food; it stretched much wider and farther than that.

Her name was Sarah. I knew she was coming that day because she contacted me that morning before she came. I didn't want any visitors, but I was being nice and accepted the fact that she would be coming to my house later. I got dressed for the first time in days. I did my hair and put on some makeup. I had been struggling, like really, really struggling. The postpartum anxiety and depression that ransacked me with my first child was on a steady climb right back to my mind. I saw her coming to the door through the big glass front windows carrying an armful of food. I picked up my baby and went to the door. I opened it just as she smiled at me. I had seen her a few times, but she didn't know me. She talked to me just a minute and left a whole meal for my family. She didn't want to leave me with words; she wanted to leave me with love. I don't even remember what she said when she was there. She didn't ask for anything in return. She didn't want any money. She didn't want any praise. She just wanted me to feel that someone was thinking of me. She said that she was praying for me. For me? But she didn't even know me.

I cried when she left. I stood there staring at the food on my counter with my brand-new baby in my arms and I cried. She was so kind to me without even knowing how I would respond to her kindness. But, honestly, I do not think she was concerned with how I would respond. She had a job of loving to do and she was going to do it no matter how she was perceived. She was what Jesus looks like. She was carrying the message of kindness to every soul she could reach. She will never know that I prayed that morning for some help. She will never know how I pleaded with the Lord just that morning for some encouragement to keep going. I just wanted to feel Him with me. She will never know the impact that her kindness had on me. She will never know that at the very moment she came, Satan was telling me I would never be a good-enough mom. He was telling me I would be a failure. He was telling me that I was in over my head.

The moment before she smiled at me, I was on the verge of a meltdown, a meltdown I could feel welling up in my heart, a meltdown that might have been the beginning of an awful next few months or even years. I was being deceived by the enemy, sinking in lies that were filling my soul. Then she rang the doorbell and changed the course of not just my day but my months ahead. Over the next few months when I was lied to by my enemy, the Lord reminded me of Sarah: if I was loved enough that He would send someone to me to show me kindness, He must love me more than I will ever know. He must be hearing me. He must be planning things on my behalf before I even know something needs to be planned. He must really love me. I will live in that truth. As you can see, I still live there. I have not forgotten, nor will I ever forget that He sent someone to me to lift me up when I needed it most. She didn't post on social media all the kind things that she was doing that day. She didn't want a pat on the back. She didn't need any of that. She didn't have a thought in her mind that day about herself. She was only thinking of others. She was kind and she didn't care if anyone but myself saw it. That is kindness in all of its intended heavenly glory.

The Choice Is Not Ours

If we are to live by His example of love and kindness and mold our lives around that, then why do we get to choose who sees it? If the Lord loves us no matter what, then why do we not show others that same love? How wonderful it is to know that even if we make the wrong choice, there will be nothing that could separate us from the love of Christ? Romans 8:35 says this truth, "Who shall separate us from the love of Christ? Shall trouble or hardship or persecution or famine or nakedness or danger or sword?" What should separate you from His love? There is nothing. What should separate you from showing His love to all people? Nothing. The enemy would have you to believe something entirely different than this truth. I hope and pray that you rest in the promises that the Lord has given you about His love. His love never fails. Show that love. "Give thanks to the Lord, for He is good. His love endures forever" (Psalm 136:1). His love is true and pure. Show that. His love is enduring. Show that. This is His definition of love: "Love is patient, love is kind. It does not envy, it does not boast, it is not proud. It does not dishonor others, it is not self-seeking, it is not easily angered, it keeps no record of wrongs. Love does not delight in evil but rejoices with the truth. It always protects, always trusts, always hopes, always perseveres" (1 Corinthians 13:4–8). I want to be kind enough to give out *His* love and I do not get to choose who I hand over that love to. I want to give that out without wanting any praise. I want to be the kindness that people pray to see. I want to be kind to *all* people so that they see that love. I want that love to flow from me freely. Even if the person I am around would never reciprocate that love or kindness, I have a duty and responsibility to show people Christ's love.

Kindness Defines Us

I desire to have a heart like Jesus. I desire for people to see in me a kind of love they have never experienced. I want people to think my level of kindness is crazy. If we really are not treating everyone like Christ would, then why do we do what we do? Why do we say what we say? Can you imagine if Christ held all of His love inside and didn't give it away? Where would we be today? If Christ didn't first love us more than His life itself, He would've never died on the cross. And, if He never died on the cross, we would forever be apart from God. That love that He showed you on the cross you may have never seen before you met someone that followed Him. Maybe the kindness that someone showed you is a kindness that you have never experienced before. If you have ever met someone that was so kind and loving and didn't need to be, you will forever have that memory. Kindness and love stick out, a type of kindness and love above and beyond. Are you known for loving like Christ? Does your attitude reflect the fact that Jesus died and showed you supreme love? I know it may seem like I am stressing how important loving is and you are correct, I am stressing it! It is the one most important thing that you can do as a Christian.

We Should Be Reflecting Christ

I can clearly see Him molding me to look like Him over the years. I can clearly see Him chipping away at all the layers of callousness the world heaped on me. I can clearly see He loves me enough to allow me to desire only Him. I am kind enough to show people that love He showed to me. I will go out of my way to show that love, the love that set me free, the love that broke the lock off my iron heart toward humanity. I will show others to help them. I will show others so they can live free. I will show others this kindness because He first showed me. Who does it benefit if I accept His kindness and then lock it all away for just myself to enjoy? That is selfishness at its finest. If I keep His kindness to myself and hide it away, it helps no one, it affects no one, and it turns no hearts to Him. I refuse to be the reason that people never come into contact with His kindness.

Listen, I have been changed by the love of Christ. I mean to say that my heart now looks nothing like it did before I knew the love of Jesus. I was raised in church. I knew the Lord from an early age. But I didn't *know* the Lord like I do now. I did not love Him like I do now. He rescued me from the chains that enemy would have had me in forever. Now I see things differently because He showed me His love.

That change in how I see love is evident in my prayers for my children. These children that I have, I have them to raise them up to be lovers of Jesus and to grow them to be leaders for His kingdom. I do not desire that they go to college to land a high-paying career; I pray that they solely desire the will of the Lord in their life. If that means that they move to a different country to work for Jesus, my heart would sing with joy. Just like I pray for them, I also now pray for myself that I would fall deeper in love with Christ. I pray that I would dwell in His presence all the days of my life. I pray that I would be able to hear His voice speaking truth to me over the lies of my enemy. I pray that my life is solely used for the cause of Christ. I simply do not see life the same way as before I was rescued.

I do not tell you all this about myself to build myself up. I do not desire a pat on the back or a job well done from anyone. I tell you all this to give you the hope that He has given to me. I tell you my story in great hope and prayer that you will rise with Jesus and triumph over your life. I desire for you to love others so deeply because you first felt the overwhelming, life-altering, never-be-the-same love of Christ. I want Him to restore relationships around you and bring new people in for His plans of good for you. I do not want you to compare yourself to anyone. At the beginning of my journey with Christ, I compared myself to everyone. As I grew and matured in my faith, I soon realized that the things that the Lord has planned for me are not the plans He has for anyone else. He will use my story and your story to make us distinctly one of a kind. There is no one else that can do what He has planned for you. There is no one else that can walk the path that He has planned for you to walk. My walk will not look the same as your walk. My place in this world is not the same as your place in it. Your pastor was called to preach, and even though you might be called to work in the nursery, the two roles serve the same purpose: spreading the love of Jesus. The place that the Lord has raised me to stand is not the place that you will be raised to stand. There is a spot waiting for you to rise to the occasion of living life in freedom and serving Christ. There is no one else that can stand in your spot. There is no one else that can use your story to bring hope. There is no one else that can write the rest of your days. The Lord will call and beckon you out of the waters, but He will not make you choose His ways. He will not make you love Him like you should. He will not make you turn from the ways of the world and follow Him. And, you are all so fortunate to have someone that chooses to love you, despite all your wrong, your sin, your lies, your deceit, your callousness, your despair, your tongue, your hate, your denial, your pride, and your shame. He loves you enough to accept all of you and then walk with you while you learn how to be more like Him. Don't stop at the choosing part and then stop walking with Him.

His Love Changes <u>E</u>verything

This love, this true love, it changes the very nature of the human heart. This love, it drives out all fear and gives peace and joy beyond all understanding. But this love requires full-fledged, no excuses, no looking back, no entertaining the ways of the world, no sitting idly on the fence of faith, and no allowing the enemy to squelch your love for Jesus Christ. This love requires you to be a true, devoted, selfless, and surrendered follower of Jesus. It requires you to be willing to give up everything to follow Him. This love requires death to self. It requires you to submit to His plan for your life. This love that you have been given requires you to give it to others whether they deserve it or they do not. Love, my friends, makes the difference between life and death. The love that was first shown to you changed your life. It gave you salvation, hope, and unity with God. That same love is not meant to be hidden in the church pews on Sundays. It is not meant to be hidden in your Bible that you read every week. It is meant to be taken out of your heart and given away. It is meant to be thrown around like confetti. Let it go. Let it fly. Give as much away as you possibly can. Be kind to every soul that you meet. They could have been praying to feel loved that day. They could have been praying to know the love that you know. Desire to show everyone Christ's love through your kindness. What would our world look like if we, as children of God, made a declaration to show the love that was first shown to us? What would it look like if we allowed nothing to stand in the way of our kindness? What if there were no lines of religion, denomination, ethnicity, race, or age that stood in the way of our kindness? The freedom that the cross gave to us did not cost us a thing. The kindness that we express through that love also costs us nothing. I think it may be the time to start acting like the kindness that was bestowed upon us is the greatest gift that we have ever been given, a gift bigger than our jobs, our friends, our homes, our families, and even bigger than our very own lives. After all, if we do not have the love of Christ in our lives, then what really do we have? And if we cannot show the love of Christ to everyone in our lives, then what do we really have to give?

Conclusion

I HAVE READ AND HEARD these truths that the Lord directed me to put into this book a thousand times and there are still days that I forget. There are still days where the enemy gets the best of me and I fail. I am no different than you. But I have been changed by the blood that flowed from Calvary. I have felt the redeeming power of it in my own heart. I am a person after the very heart of God and I want you to be as well. He rescued me off the ledge and I refuse to live like I was not saved by Him. He has given me a purpose and a hope that I never imagined that I could have. I have done the research, I have sought Him out, and I know who He is, and therefore I know who I am. When I start to wonder who I am, I simply have to think of who He is: my Savior that is brave, strong and kind. In that moment, I know that He lives in me and I am much more than how I view myself. "No, in all these things we are more than conquerors through him who loved us" (Romans 8:37).

Are you aware now of who you were created to be? Are you aware of who created you? You were created by God who created the heavens and the earth! You were created by God who tells the waves where to stop! You were created by God who sent His Son to die on a cross so you could be set free! You were created by God who loves you more than you can even comprehend! You were created by God who wants you to take His hand every day and let Him lead you! He wants nothing more than to just love you! My hope is that you hear and see and feel God in a way that you never have before. My hope is that you do not live chained in a corner of life unable to defend yourself. Rise up! I am over it! I am done! Are you?

I hope you know now that you were created to be brave enough to face any circumstance. I hope you know now that you are strong enough to go through any storm holding His hand. I hope you know now that you were made kind enough to show everyone the love that was first shown to you. That love will shake the shame right out of your bones. That love will change the way you view your walk with Christ. That love will allow you to be able to walk in the truth forever. That love will show you how to love. I hope you know that the blood that was shed for you will keep running. It will run over all of your sins. It will make you whiter than snow. That blood that ran down from the cross is the same blood that makes you able to live free from the chains of this life.

The Run Back to Jesus

I am created to live victorious and so are you. I realize I will have bad days and pain will come, but that doesn't change my hope. I realize I will sin and fail Him and maybe walk out in that sea on my own from time to time, but His voice is always there calling me back to Him, calling me to see the plans He has for me, calling me to see how much He loves me. I see now that the enemy wants me to live in my circumstances forever. I have been out in that sea. I have been in that courtroom. I have seen the fork in that road. I have chosen the path that doesn't include God. I have walked away from the love God has for me because it was hard to follow Him. I have walked away because I did not feel like He even loved me anymore. But I can see clearly now what happened when I walked out on God's love because it was too hard. I can see clearly what it looked like when my enemy took my hand and thought he had won the battle. The Lord allowed me to see what that switch from truth to deception really looks like.

It was when certain circumstances came to me in life that I was being asked to walk blindly in faith with Him. It almost seemed as though I was being pummeled over and over while I held His hand through the circumstance. At some point in the hurting I doubted who's hand it was that I was holding. I could not handle any longer that a loving God would allow "this" to happen to me. I dropped

His hand. If He wouldn't stop the hurt then I was going back to being the one in control. Except as I stood there and thought about what I was doing, the enemy came up and slyly grabbed my hand. The enemy took my hand and laced his fingers through mine. It was such a fast switch I didn't even know it happened right away. I then made bad choices on my own as I walked away from Jesus. I said things I wouldn't have said had I been walking right beside Him. I did things I would not have done had He been near me, holding my hand. Then my enemy began to whisper lies to me. He convinced me God was not who He said He was and in turn I was not who He said I was. I was shamed, bitter, embarrassed, and depressed about my choices. He led me through my past where he resides. I let him lead me for far too long. I listened to him sugarcoat the lies he told me. I listened to him telling me it was okay to remain angry and bitter. He told me God wouldn't forgive what I had done. He told me everyone walked away and I was alone. He told me my past was too great to be forgiven. He told me that *God did not love me.* There it was. The greatest lie of all, the lie that makes even the strongest people fall, the lie that made me look back at all the miles I've traveled and see only myself walking, the lie that is so far from the actual truth that I failed to discern what I was even hearing. If I believed this lie, I would believe all other lies from this point on. I was going to have to make a choice. Did I believe all He said was true about who He was and in turn who I was, or did I not believe Him?

In that moment before I made my choice, I turned around to see if the Lord was even still there watching me. Was He even still there calling for me to come home? Was He even still there holding out His hand after I dropped it and unknowingly took off with my enemy? Did He even want me to come home? Did He love me enough to want me back after all I had done? I turned my head to make sure I was right about Him leaving me.

But Jesus was there. He was crying for me. He was begging me to see the lies. He was begging me to see the love that flowed from Him. I caught a glimpse of the truth. I felt just a tiny bit of His love. My soul knew the difference. I looked down at my hand locked to the enemy. I looked at myself. What was I doing? Who was I living for? Where was he taking me? In that one second, I listened to my Lord's voice calling me. I jostled my fingers loose from the enemy and I ran from him. I turned on my heels in an instant and took off toward Jesus. His arms were spread wide open waiting for me to come back. His tears were streaming down His cheeks as I ran. He was calling me home. My pace picked up as I could feel the enemy coming after me. I ran faster to Him. I literally ran with everything that was in me. I ran past all the defeat. I ran past all the circumstance of my life on earth. I ran past all the hurt. I ran past all the pain. I ran past all the lies that kept me from Him. I ran past all the people that said they followed Him but did not. I ran past the lies staked out by the enemy. I didn't even slow down as I collided into Him. He raised His mighty hand palm toward the enemy, and my enemy stopped dead in His tracks. He literally hit a glass wall put up by the Lord in that second and he stopped. He had no choice but to stop. He had no choice but to stay away from me with Him. Just like that, he was gone.

The Lord lowered His hand and hugged me. He told me He loved me. He told me I was His and He was mine. He held my face in His hands and told me the truth. He told me no matter what He'd never leave me. He told me I was brave enough to face the enemy and I was strong enough to decipher his lies. He told me I was kind enough to show others this love. Above all, He told me I was greatly loved and He showed me His hands, the proof that I was so very loved.

Get away from the enemy and his lies and break free! Run as fast as you can to the One who holds your tomorrow. Run until you collide right into Him. Run until you know you are in His arms. You are a child of the One, true God and a follower of Jesus Christ. Go live like that alone is what defines you. You are brave. You are strong. You are kind. You can live like you possess all of this. You are created to live like you possess all of these things. Go, live like it. Go, and love. Go, and be a real, victorious, mighty, truthful, dedicated, brave, strong, kind follower of Jesus. He has good plans for you.

"For I know the plans I have for you" declares the Lord, "plans to prosper you and not to harm you, plans to give you hope and a future. Then you will call on me and come and pray to me, and I will listen to you. You will seek me and find me when you seek me with all your heart." (Jeremiah 29:11–13)

The End

About the Author

KRISTIN SNOW IS A hairstylist from Terre Haute, Indiana. She never dreamed of becoming a writer but as she followed Christ, He asked her to follow Him and He chose this path for her. She is now a writer, blogger, and speaker, helping others to feel the earth-shattering, chain-breaking, true love of Christ. She talks of her freedom through Christ with gritty realness, soul-searching reflection and serious truth. She is the founder of www.bskministries.com. She lives this life with her husband and their three young children. She enjoys being outdoors on their small farm watching the corn, cows and kids growing under the Indiana sun.